Welcome to A Fun Animal Coloring Book!
In this coloring book, you'll find everything from cute pets to wild animals. It's a great opportunity to help your kids learn through the joy of coloring.
I hope you enjoy this book as much as I enjoyed creating its pages.
Thank you for supporting my art, your support motivates me to keep creating and to always give my best, bringing you more relaxing and enjoyable moments.
With love,
Angelica, from Creart.

Before you start your coloring journey, just a quick heads-up:
Amazon paper works best with colored pencils. If you're using alcohol markers or any markers that tend to bleed through, it's a good idea to place a blank sheet of cardstock or thick paper behind the page to protect the one underneath.
Now you're all set, find a cozy spot and enjoy bringing these pages to life with your colors!

Blank cardstock behind the page.

Here is the list of animals you'll find in the book: Flamingo, Pig, Sloth, Elephant, Bison, Cat, Goldfish/Fish, Horse, Hamster, Bird/Dove, Turtle, Parrot, Tiger, Rabbit, Rooster, Gecko, Giraffe, Bear, Dog, Duck, Hen, Canary, Lion, Butterfly, Wolf, Rhinoceros, Deer, Cheetah, Hippopotamus, Fox.

Follow @creartdsign on Pinterest to see coloring process videos, and fresh creative ideas to keep your imagination blooming. connect with a community that loves cozy, charming designs just like you!

© 2025 CREARTDSIGN. ALL RIGHTS RESERVED.
THIS BOOK IS FOR PERSONAL USE ONLY. NO PART MAY BE COPIED, SHARED, OR SOLD WITHOUT WRITTEN PERMISSION.
THANK YOU FOR YOUR SUPPORT!

THIS BOOK BELONGS TO

_____

_____

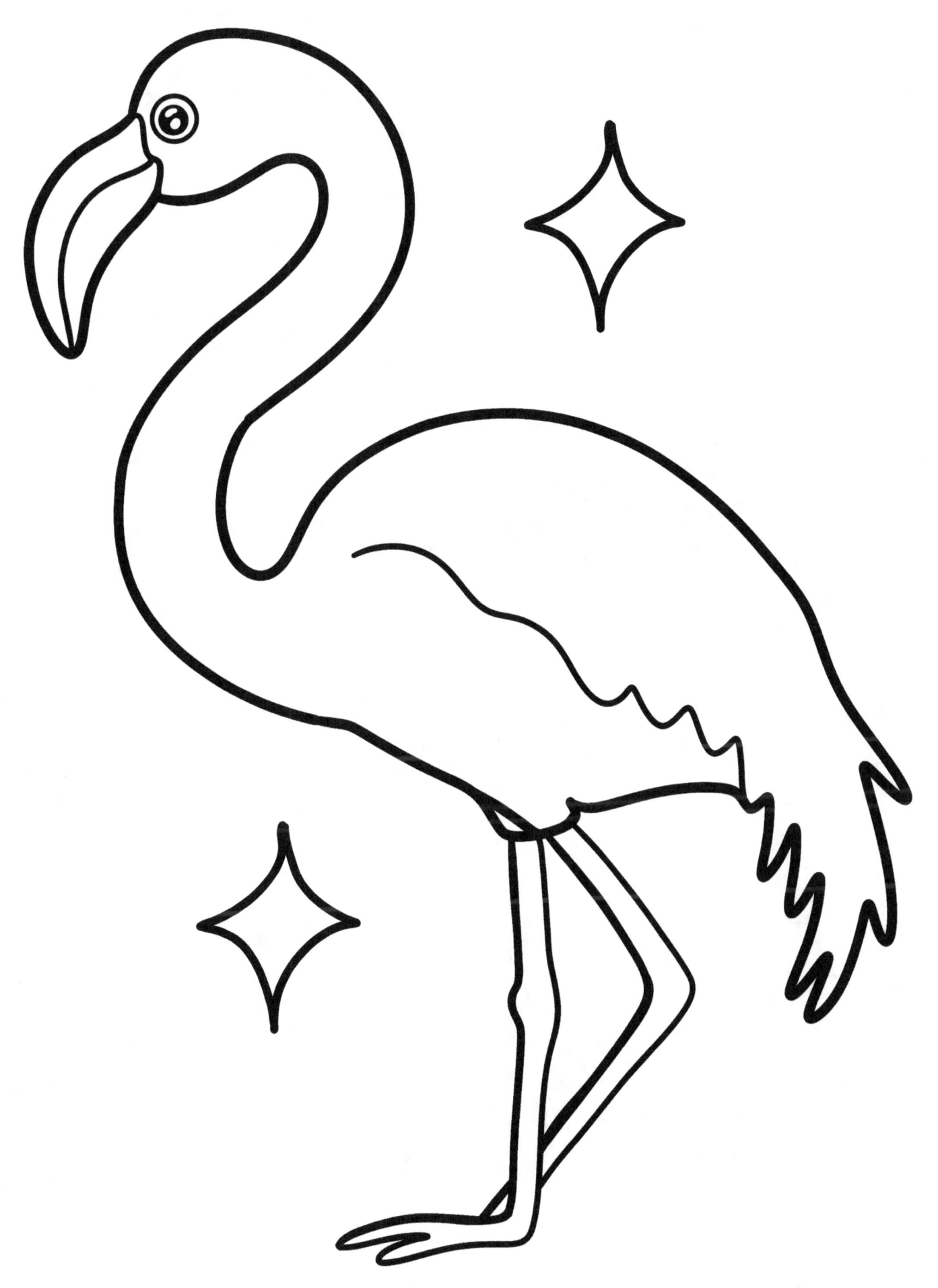

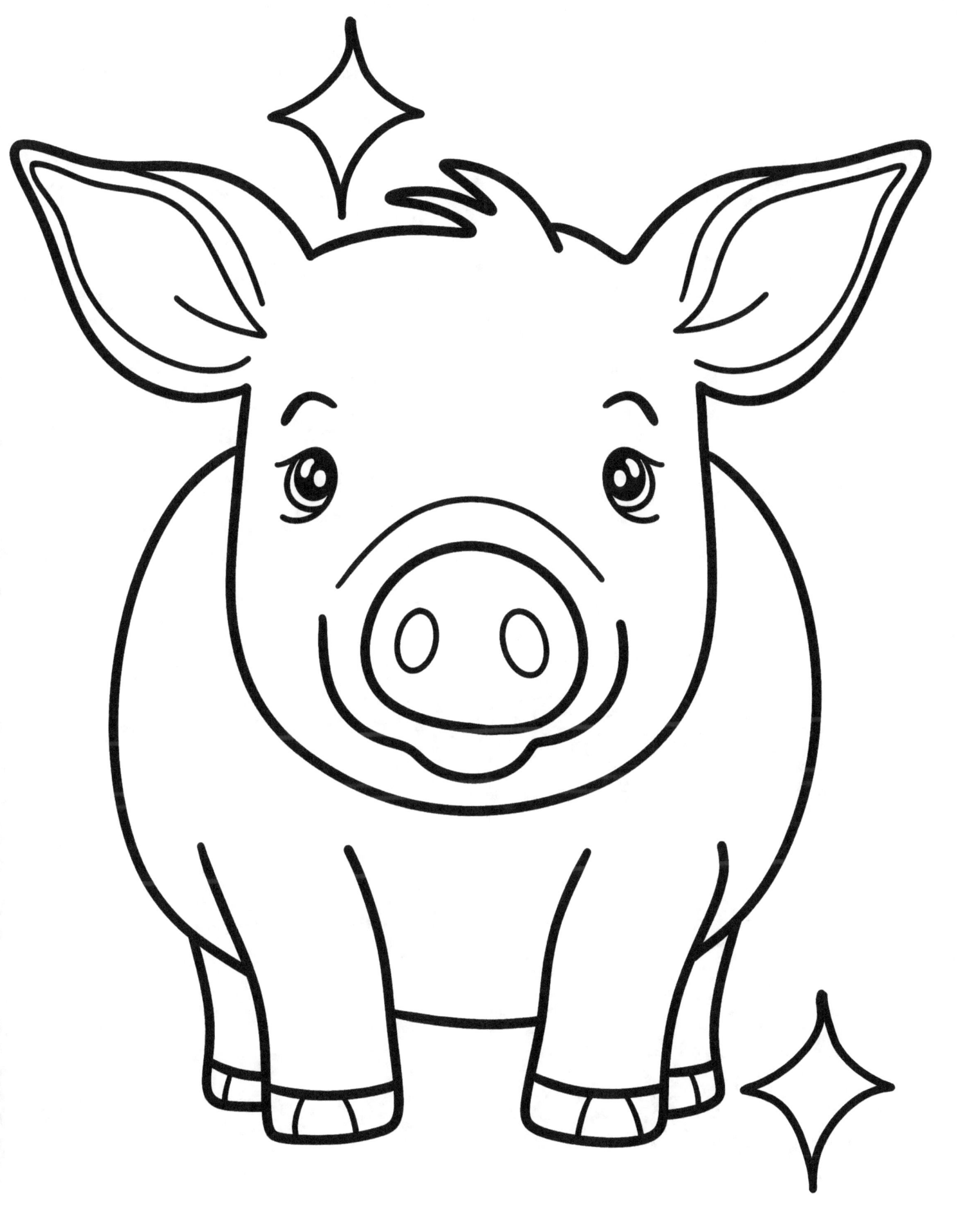

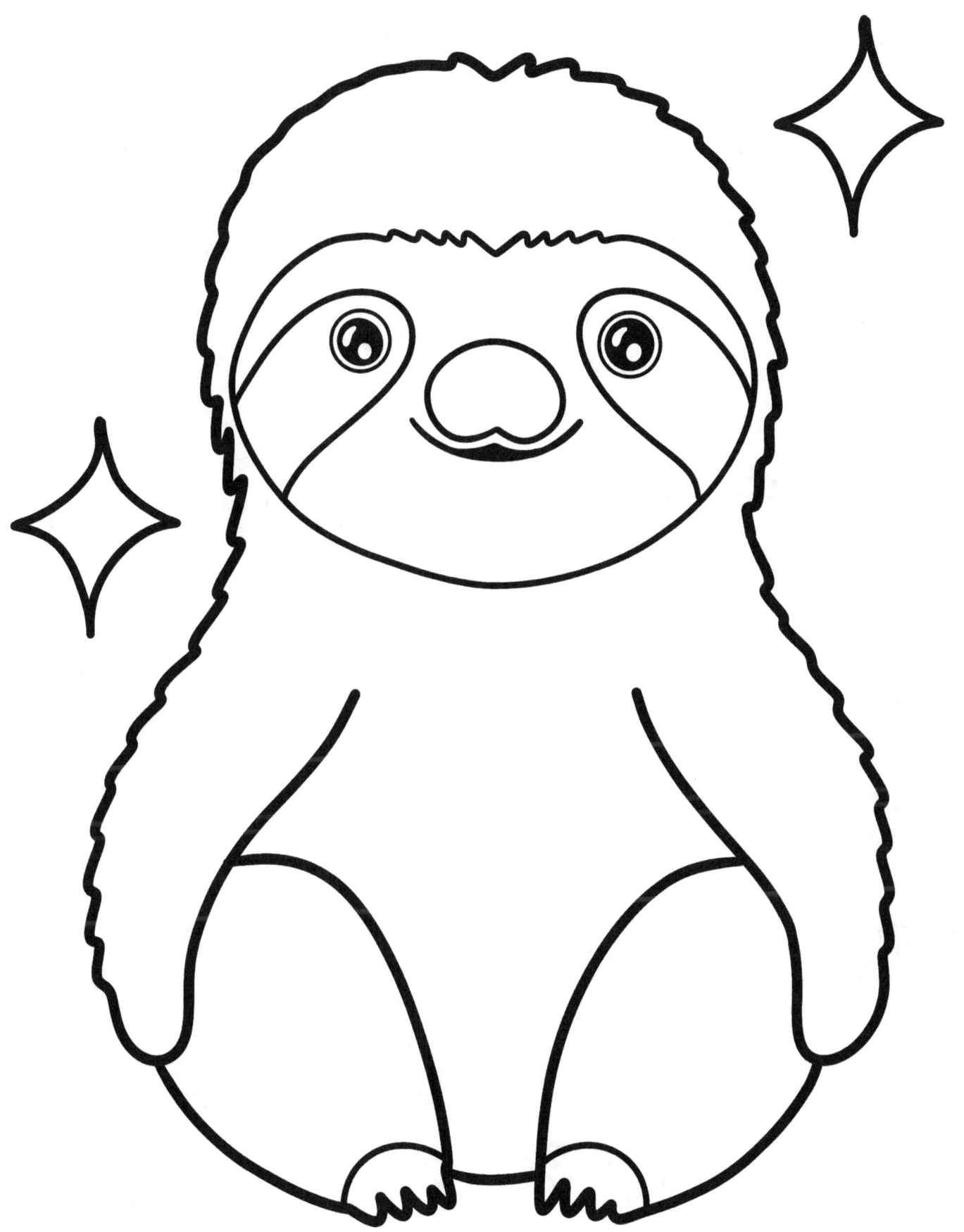

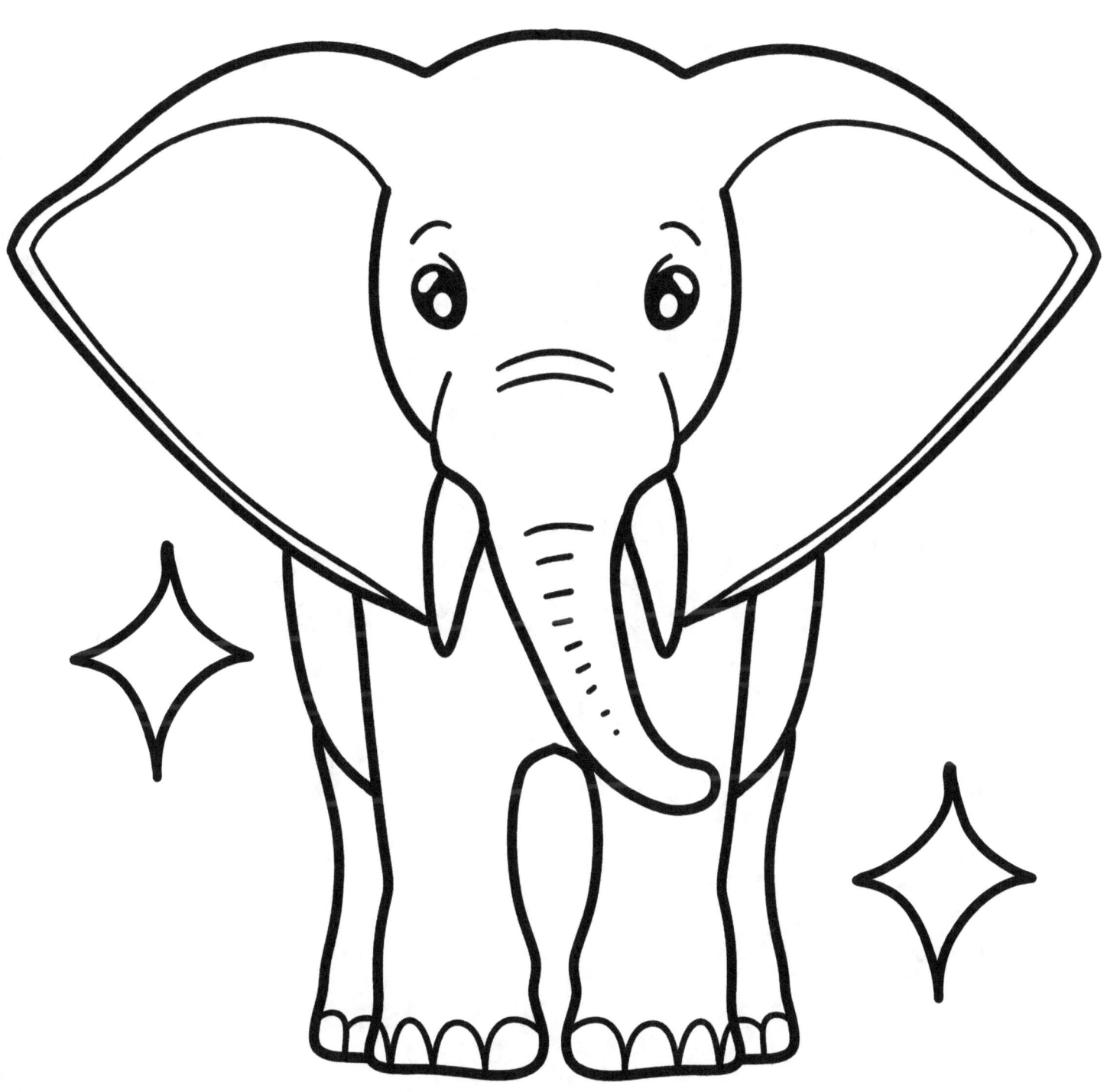

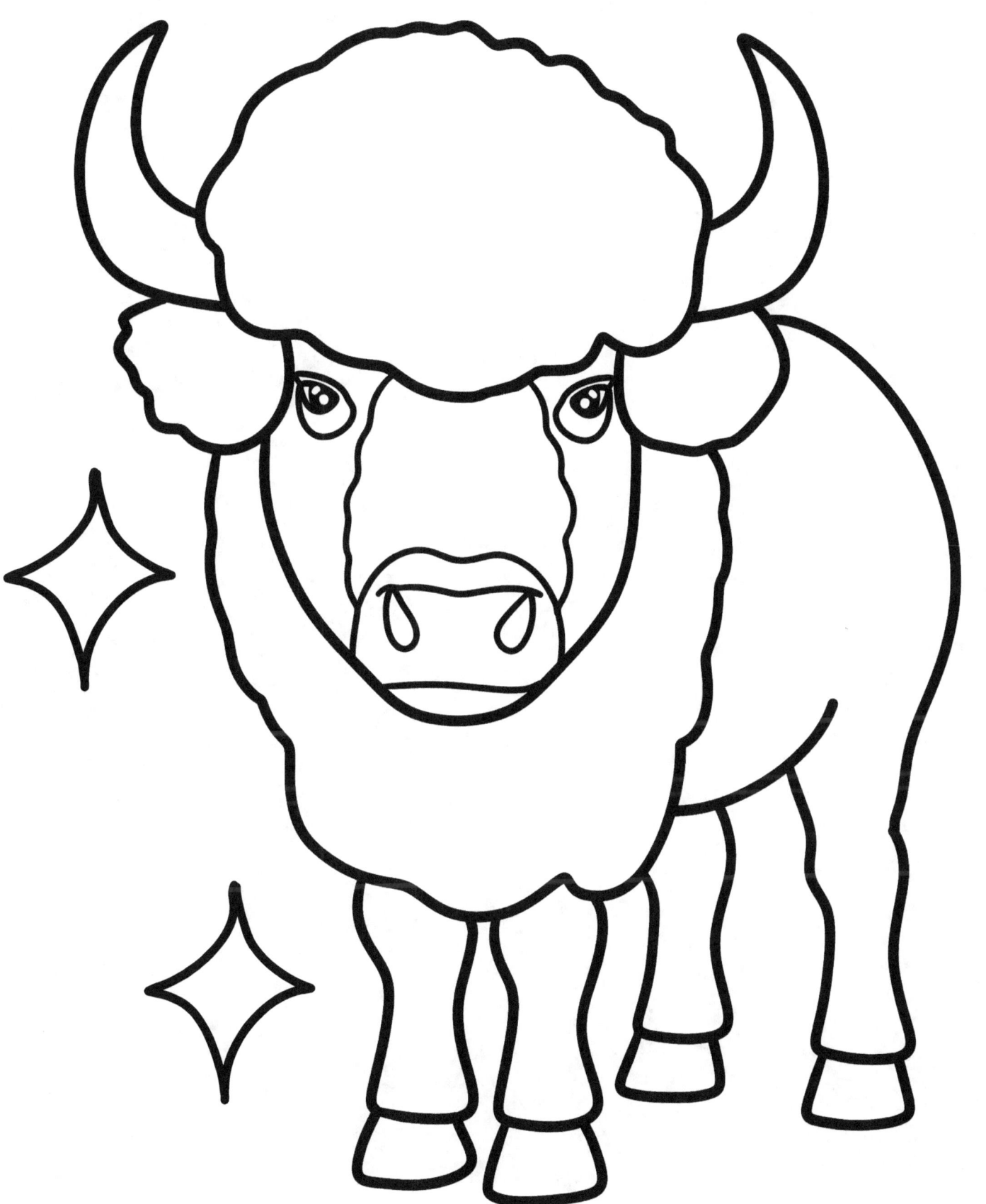

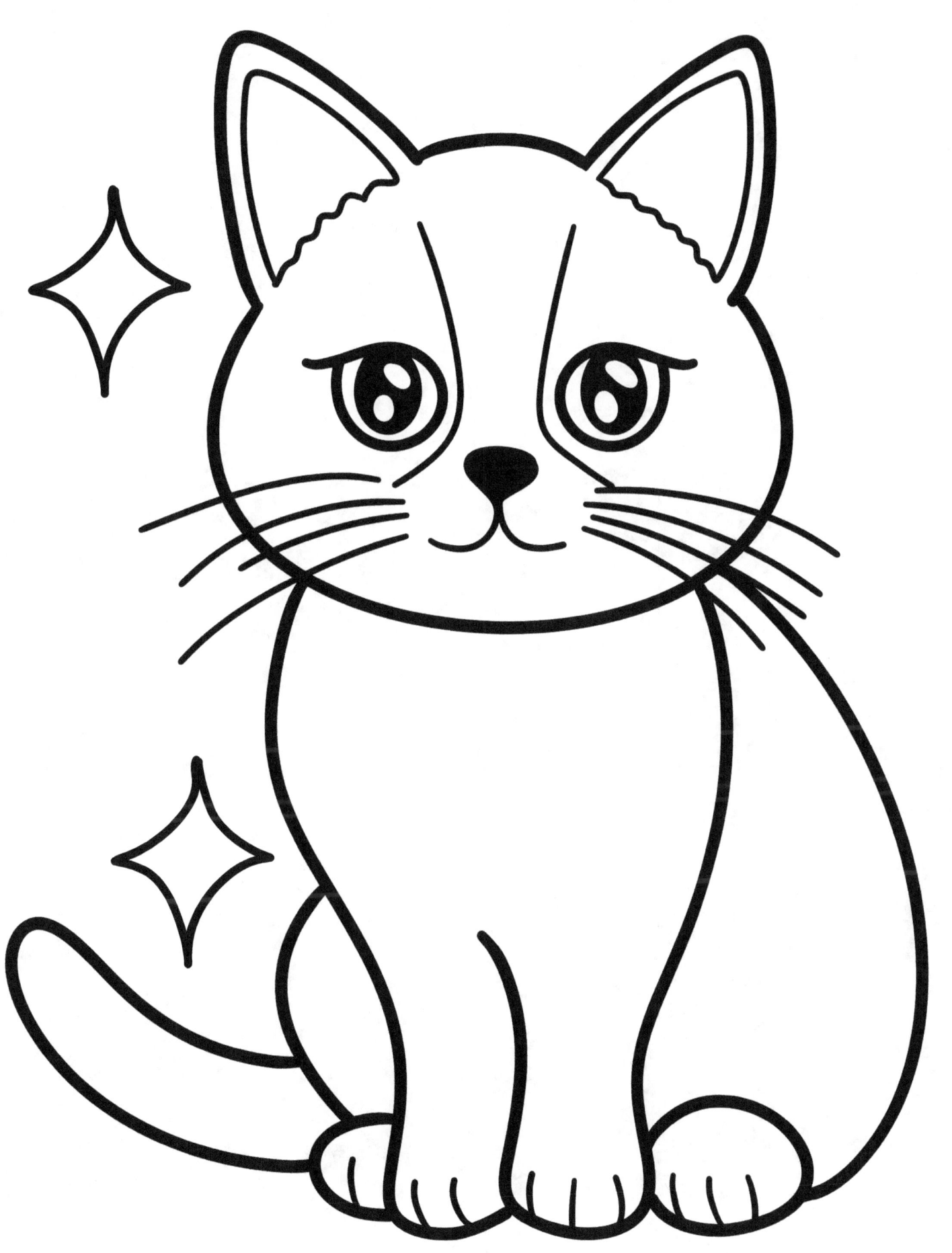

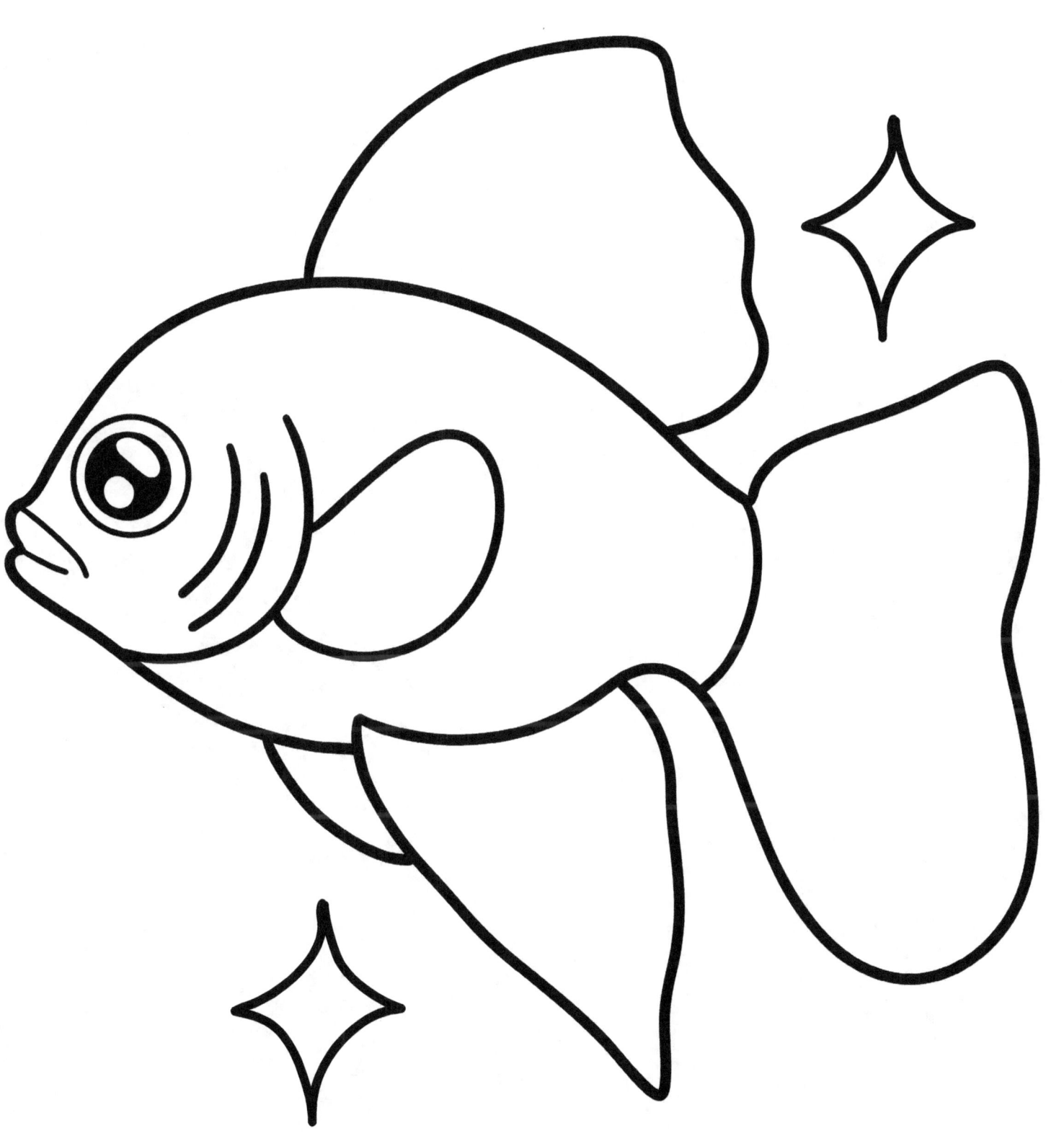

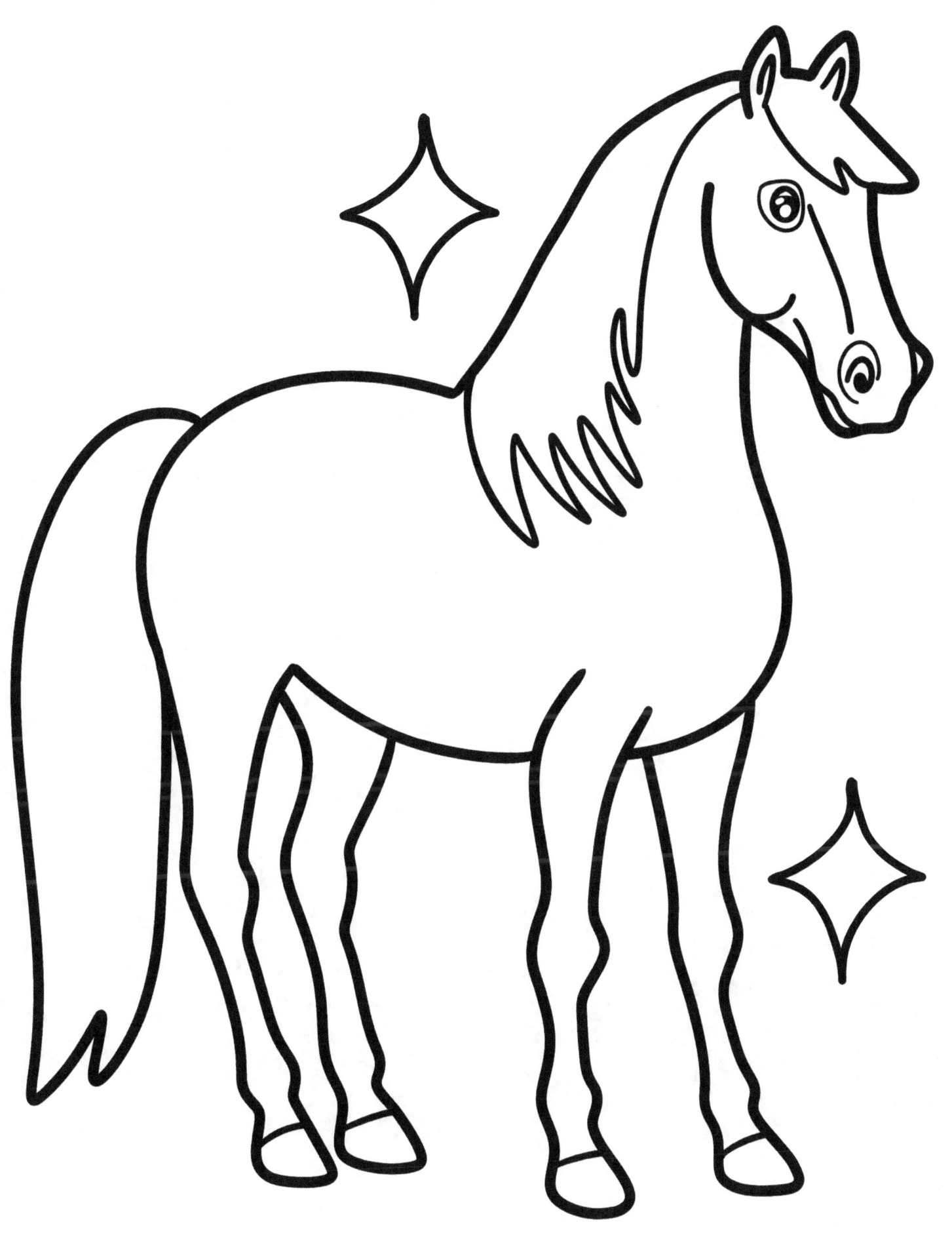

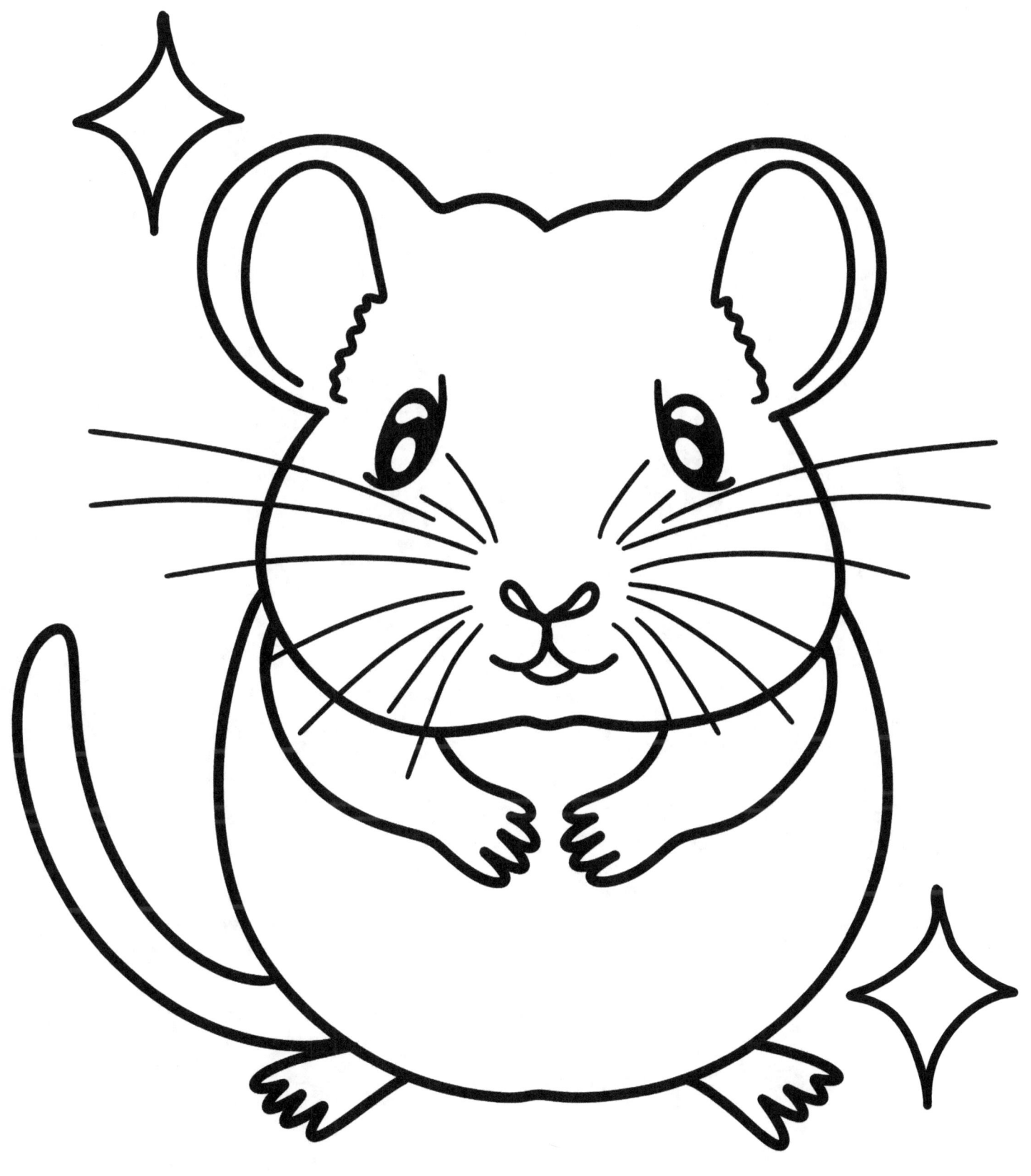

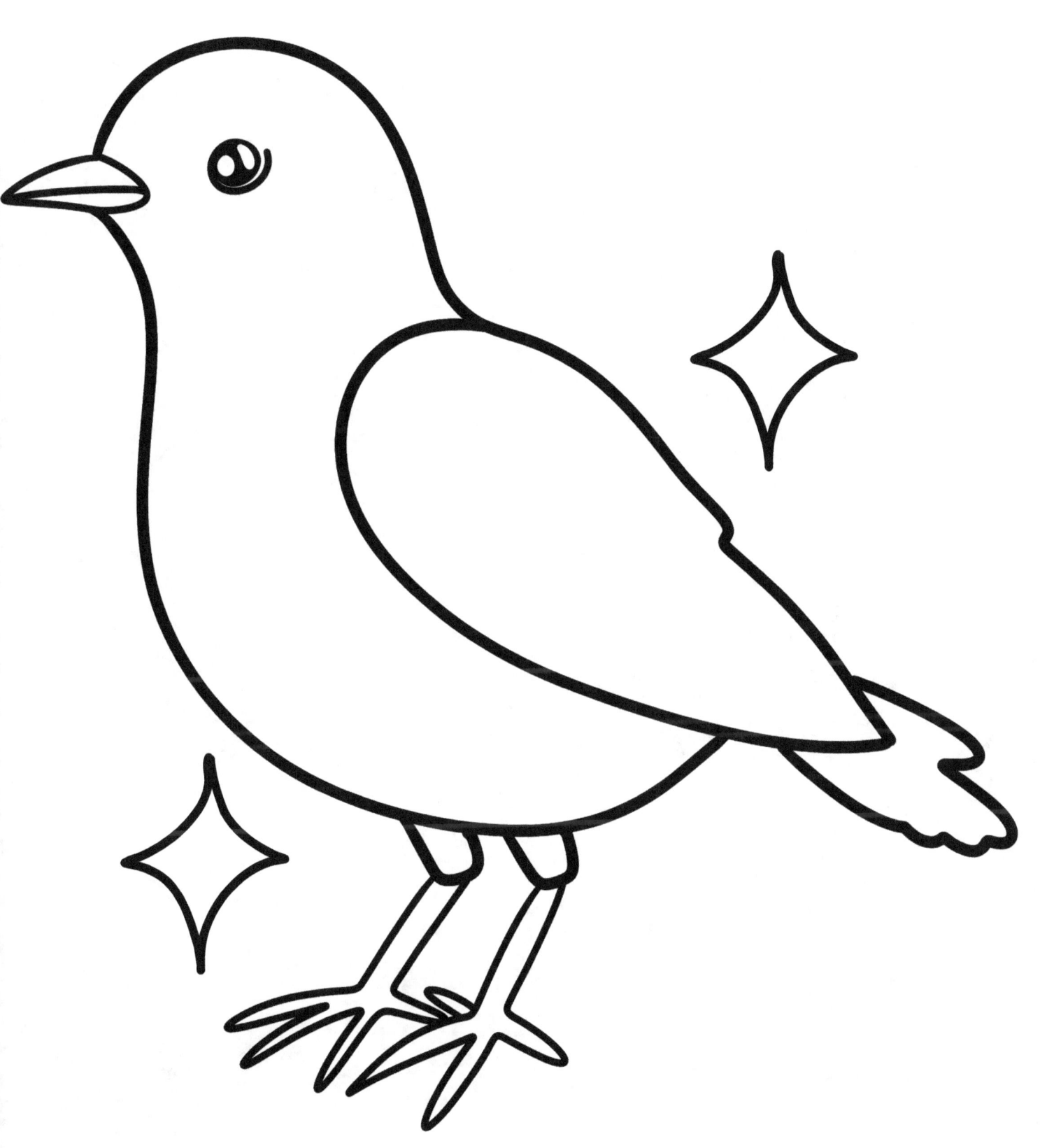

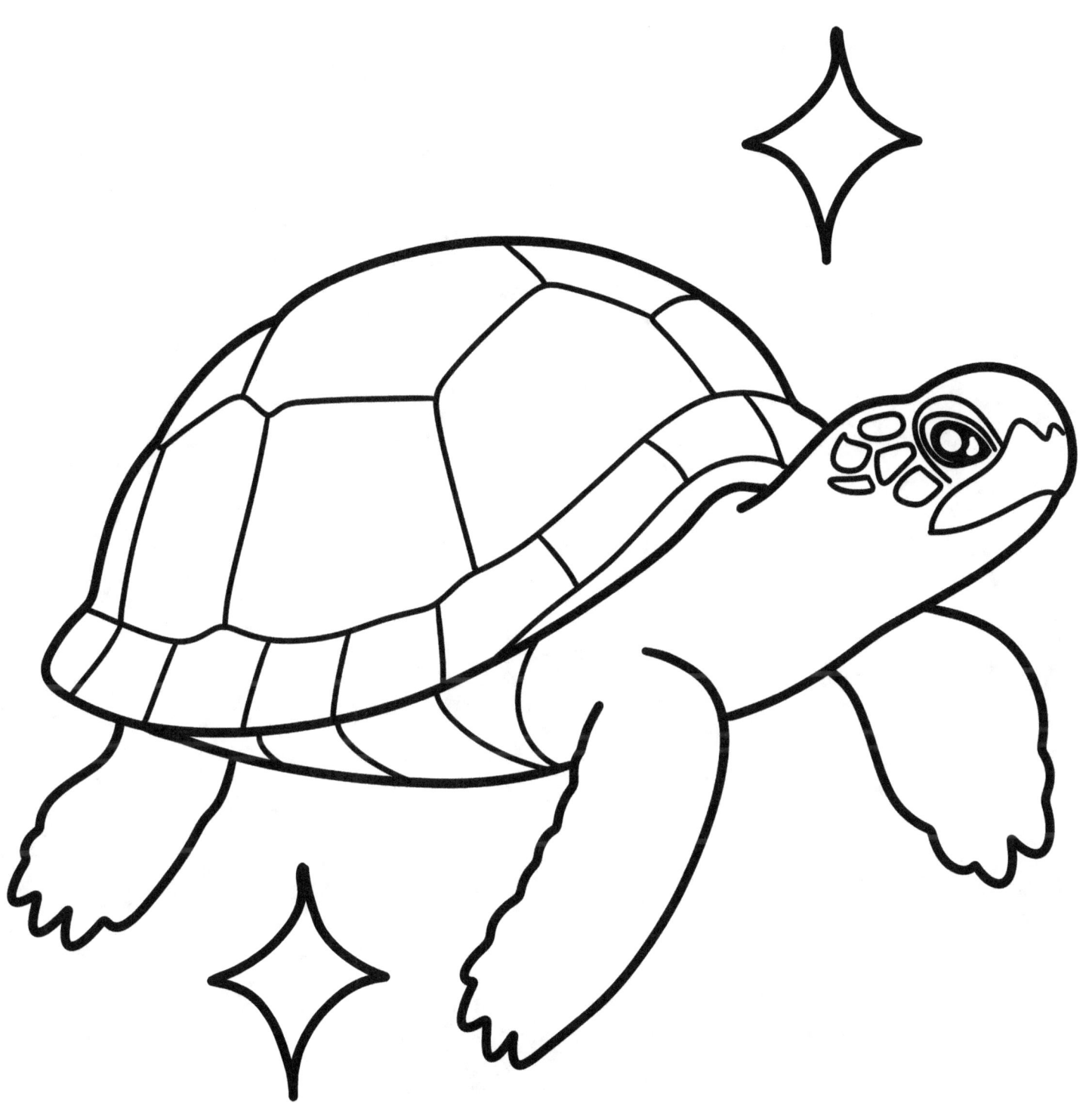

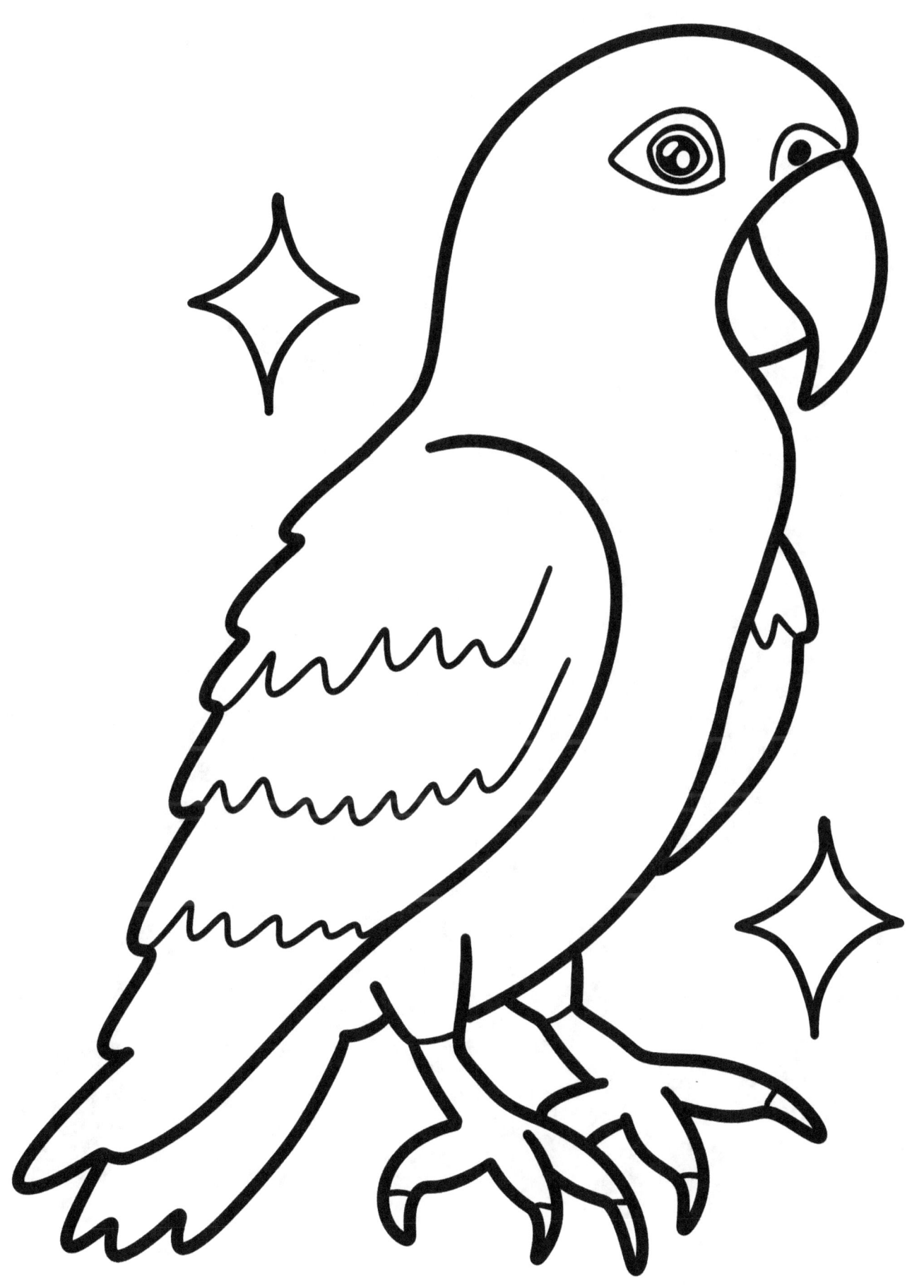

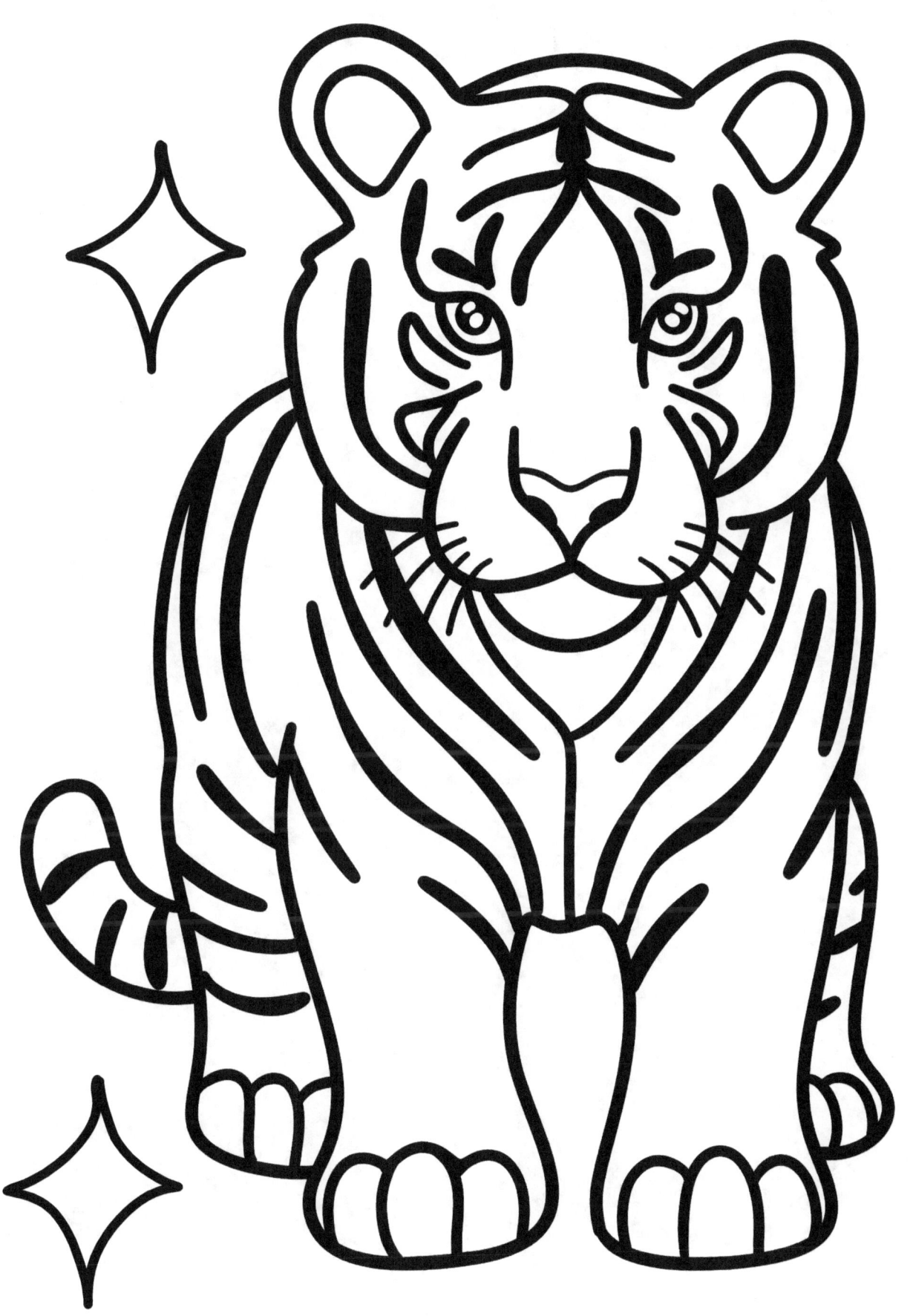

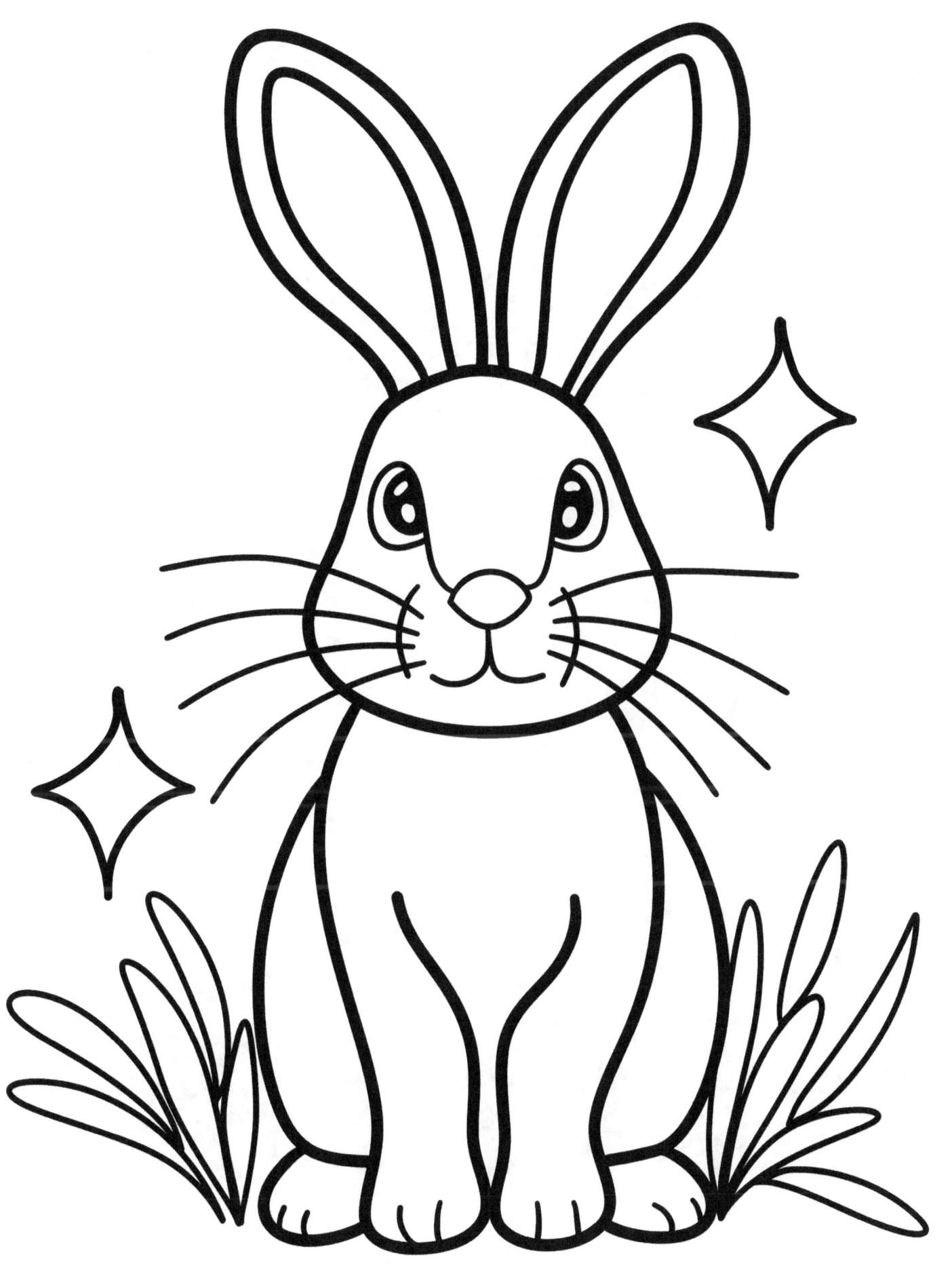

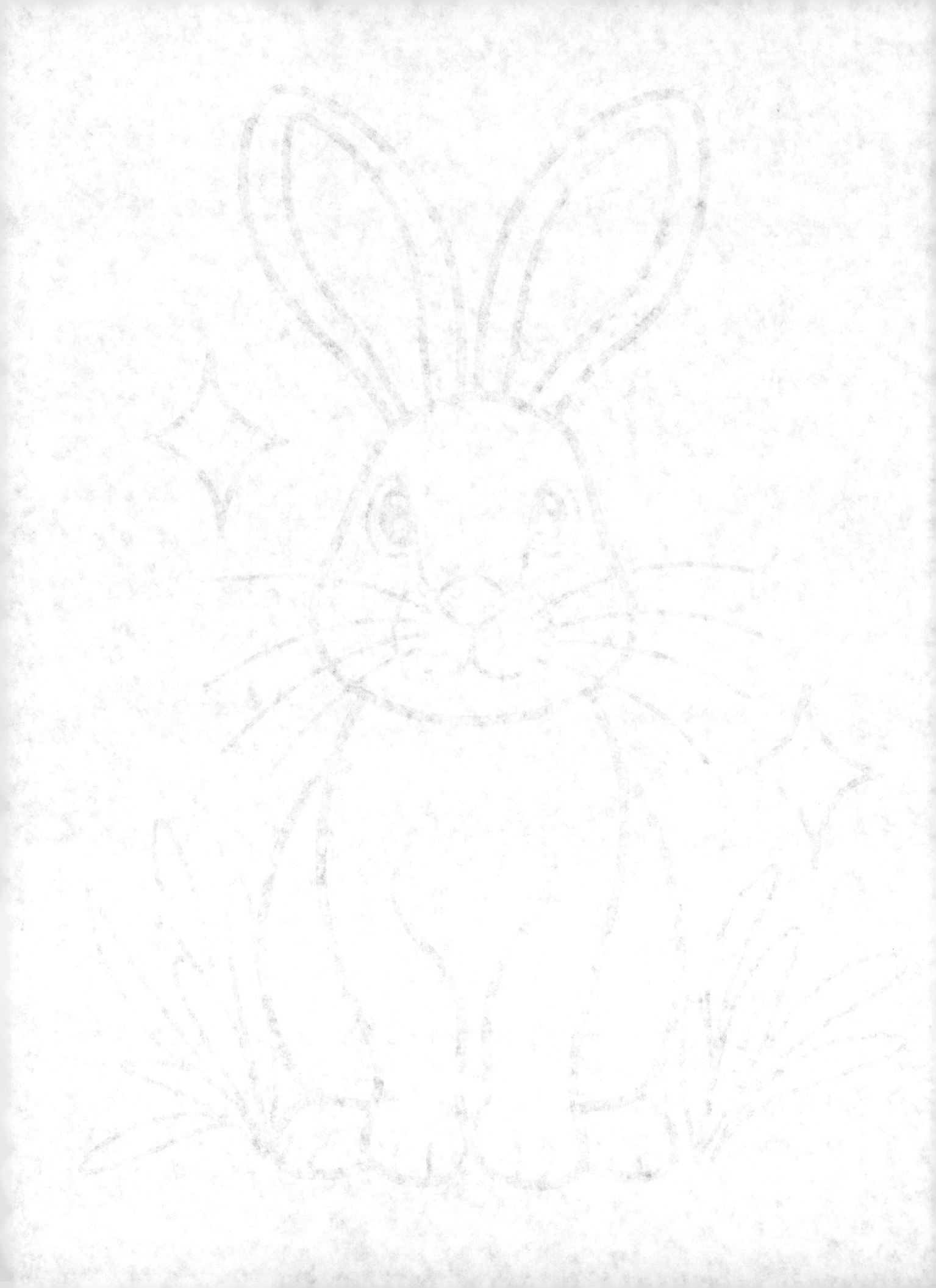

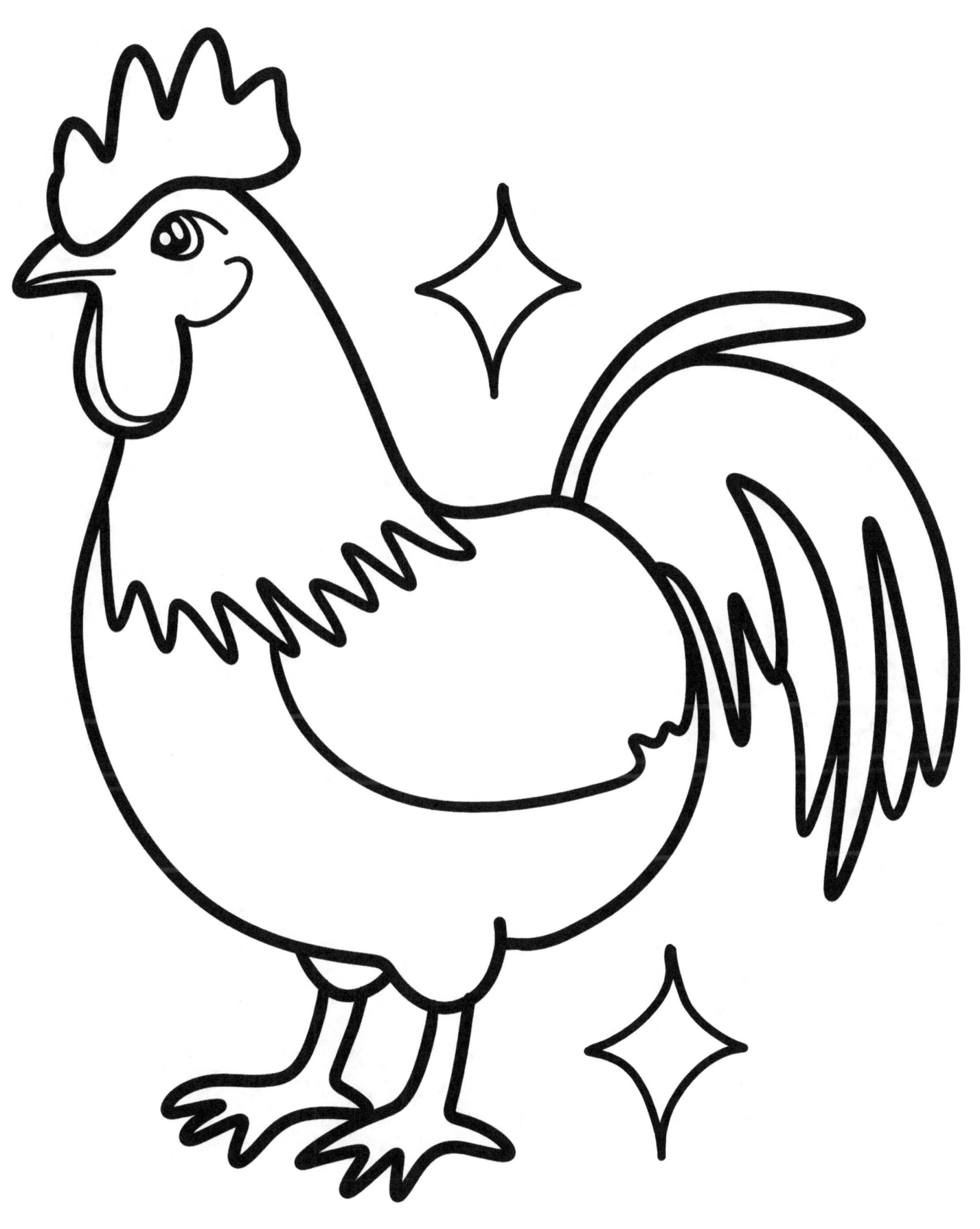

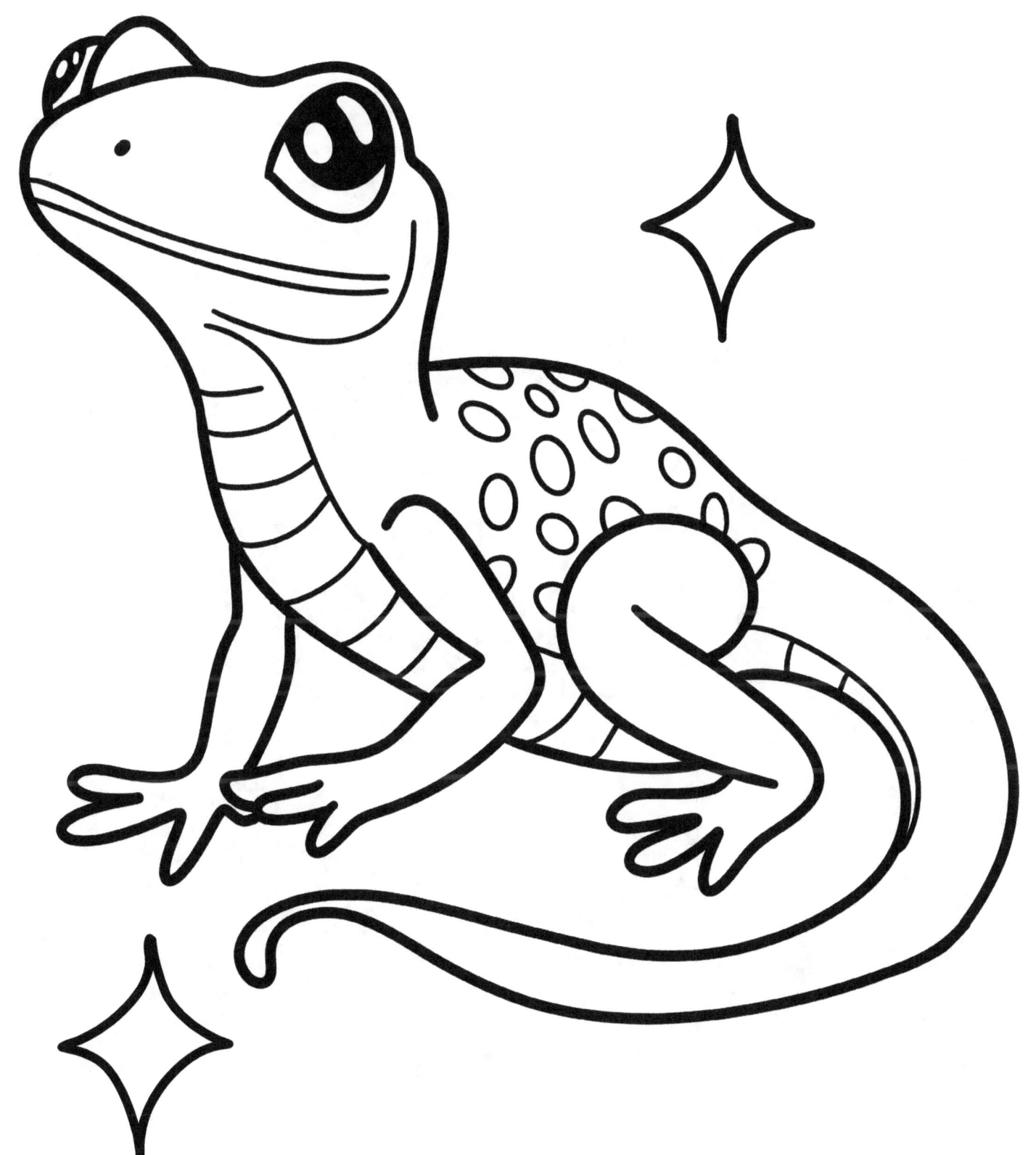

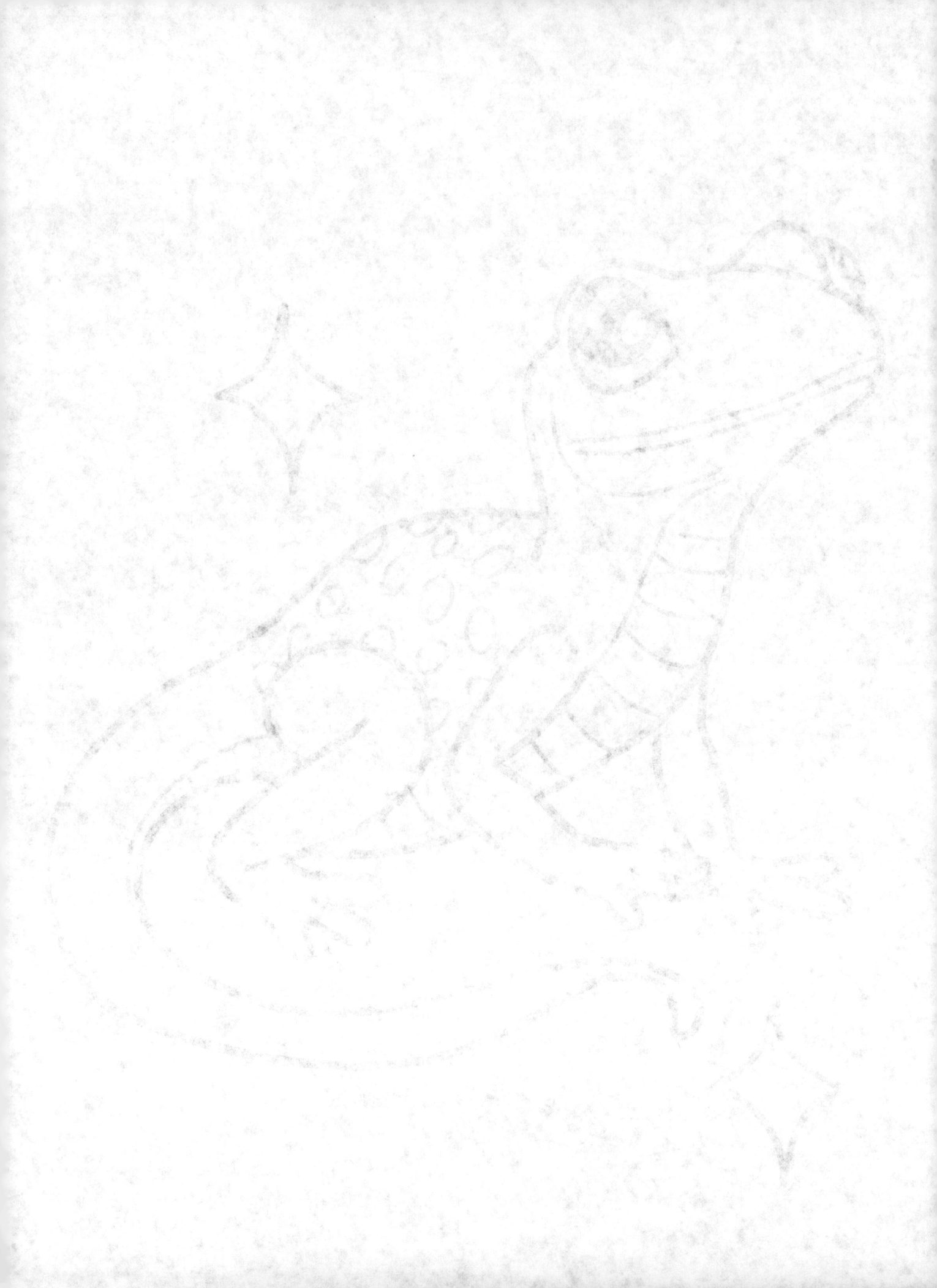

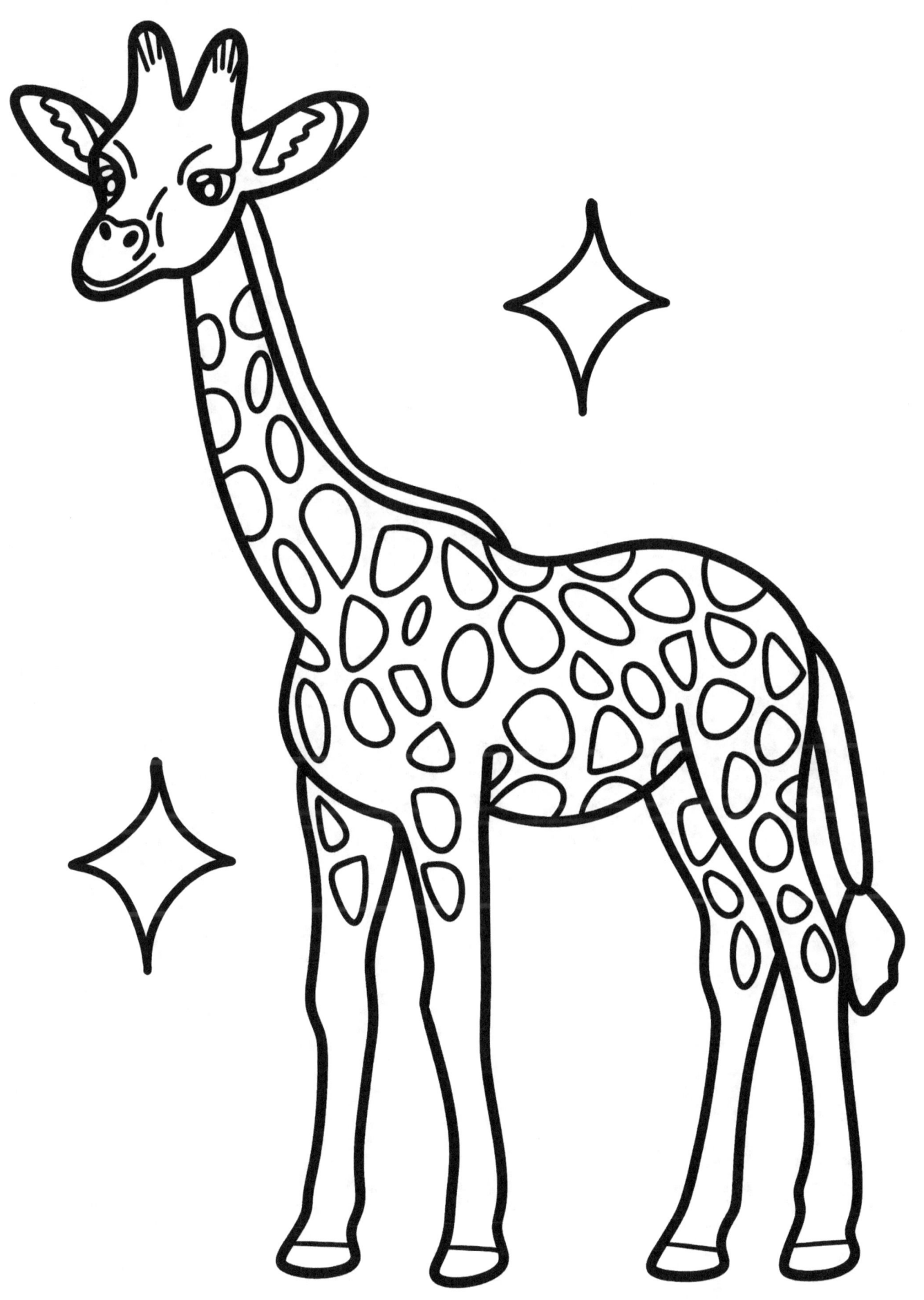

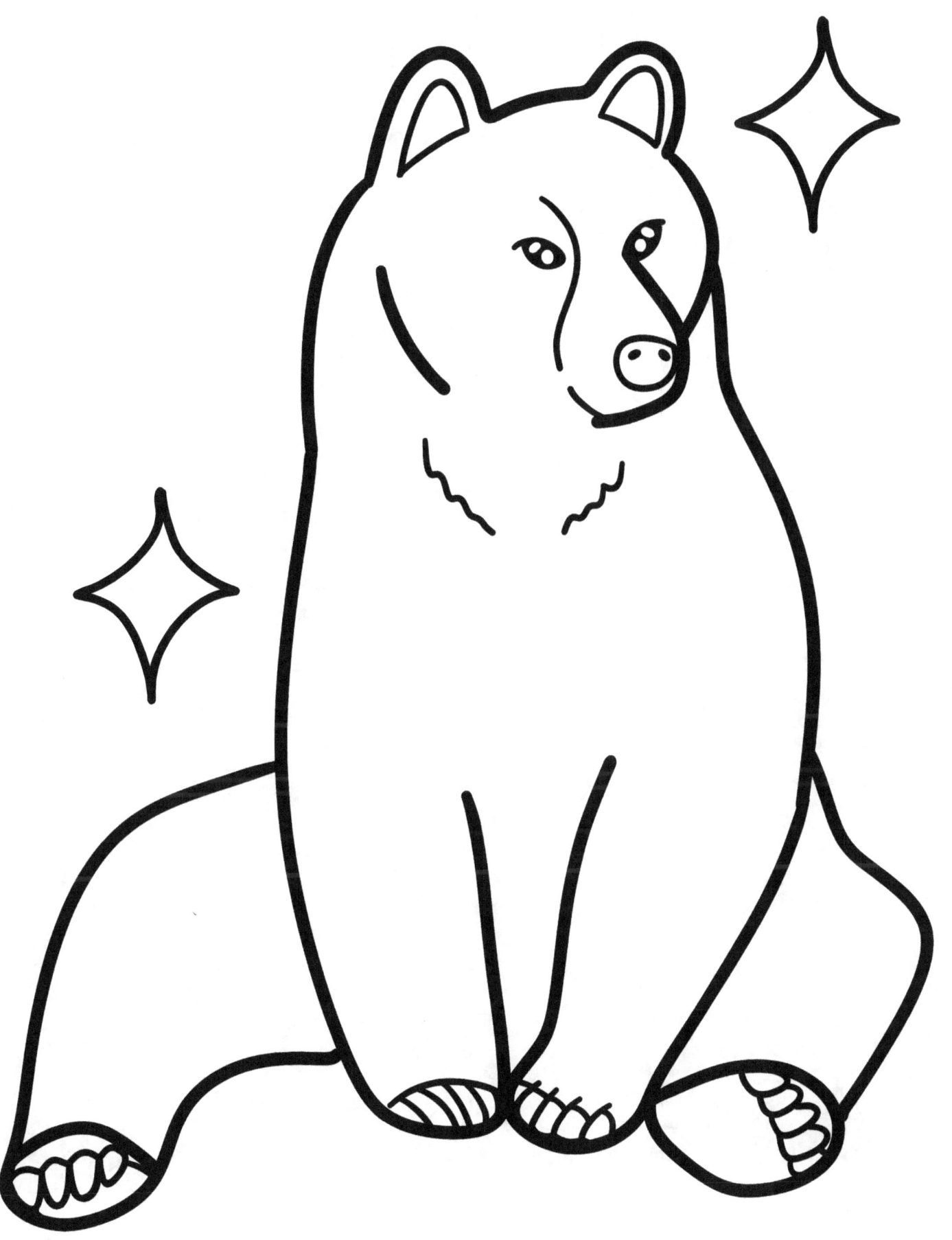

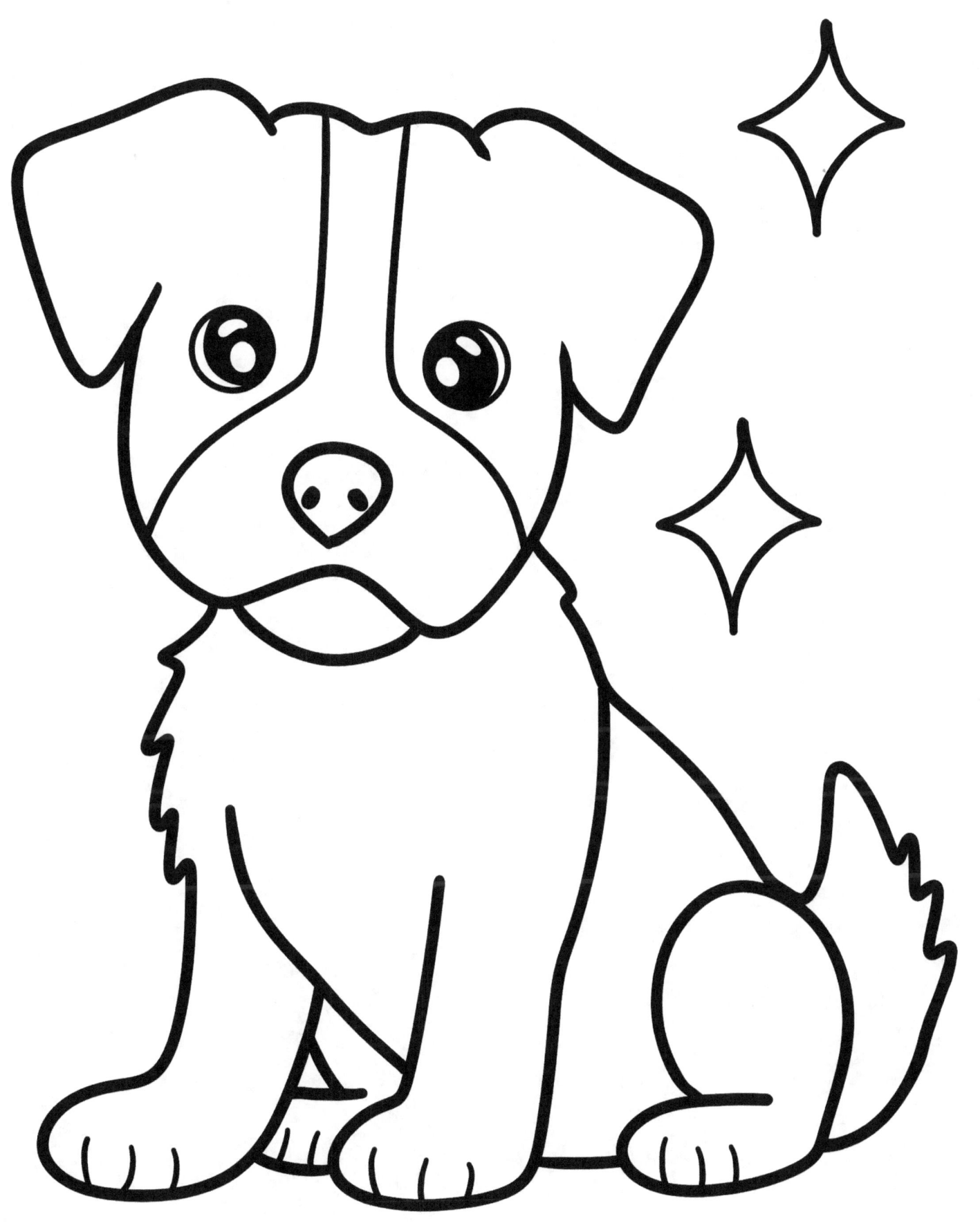

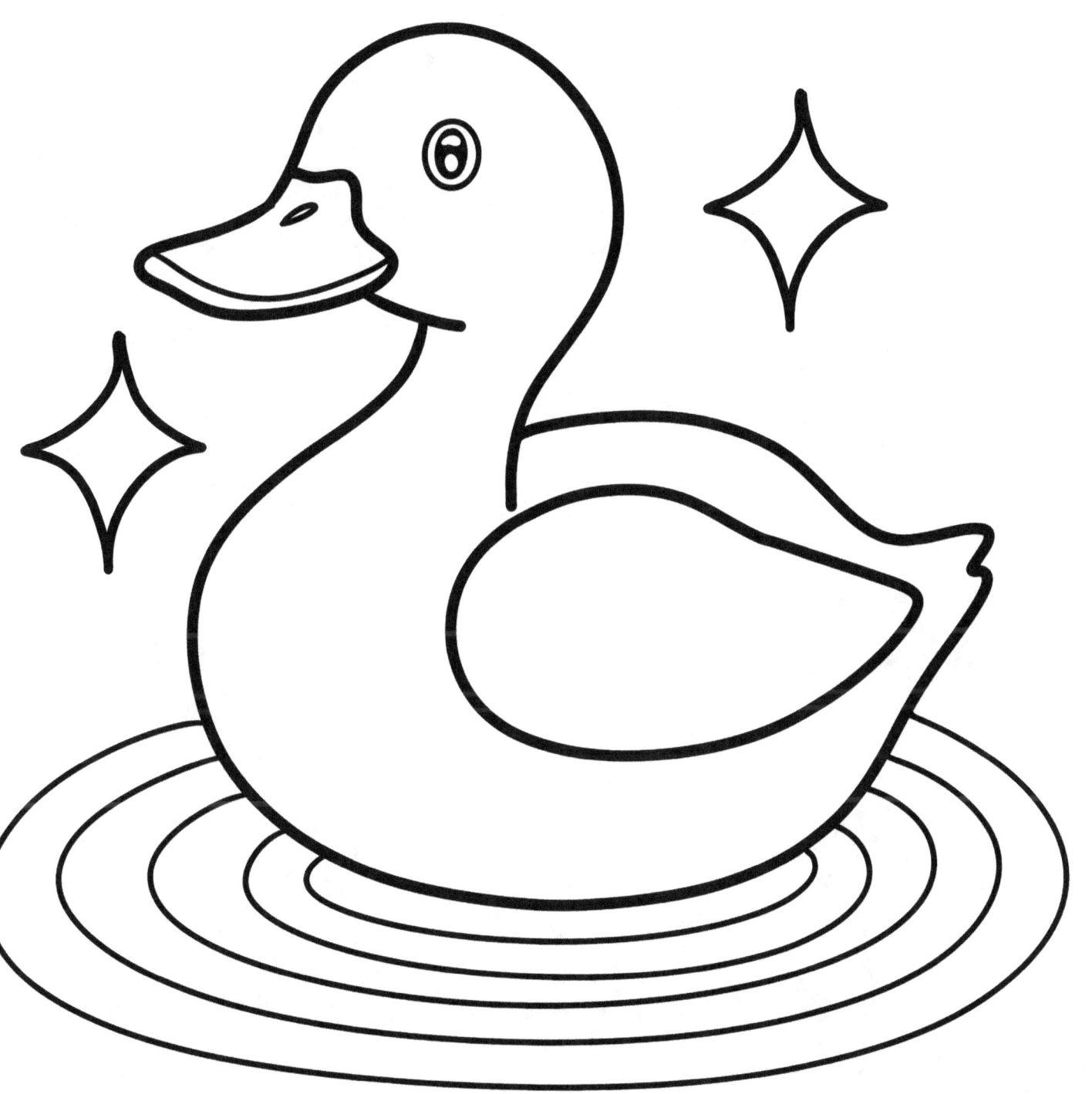

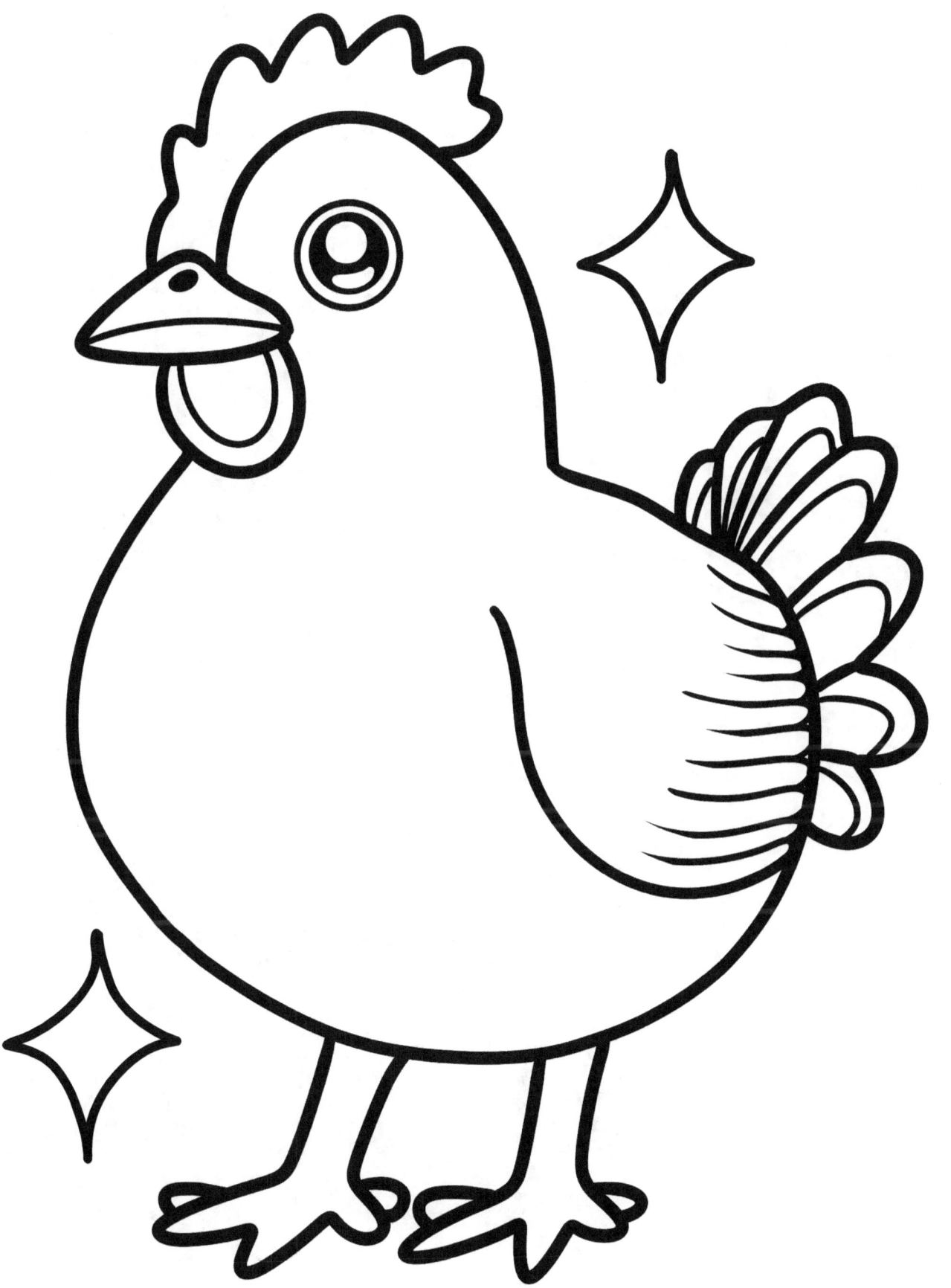

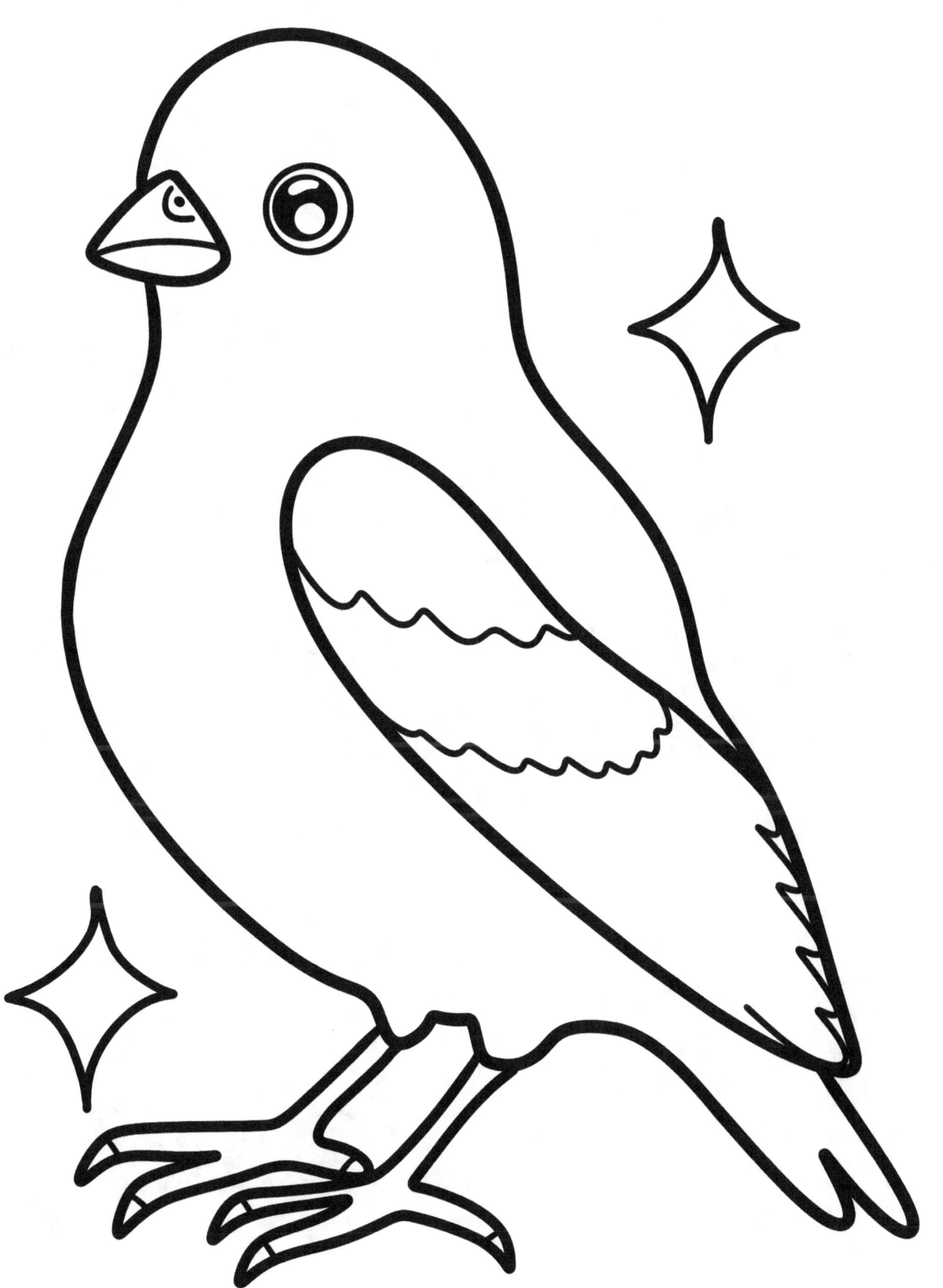

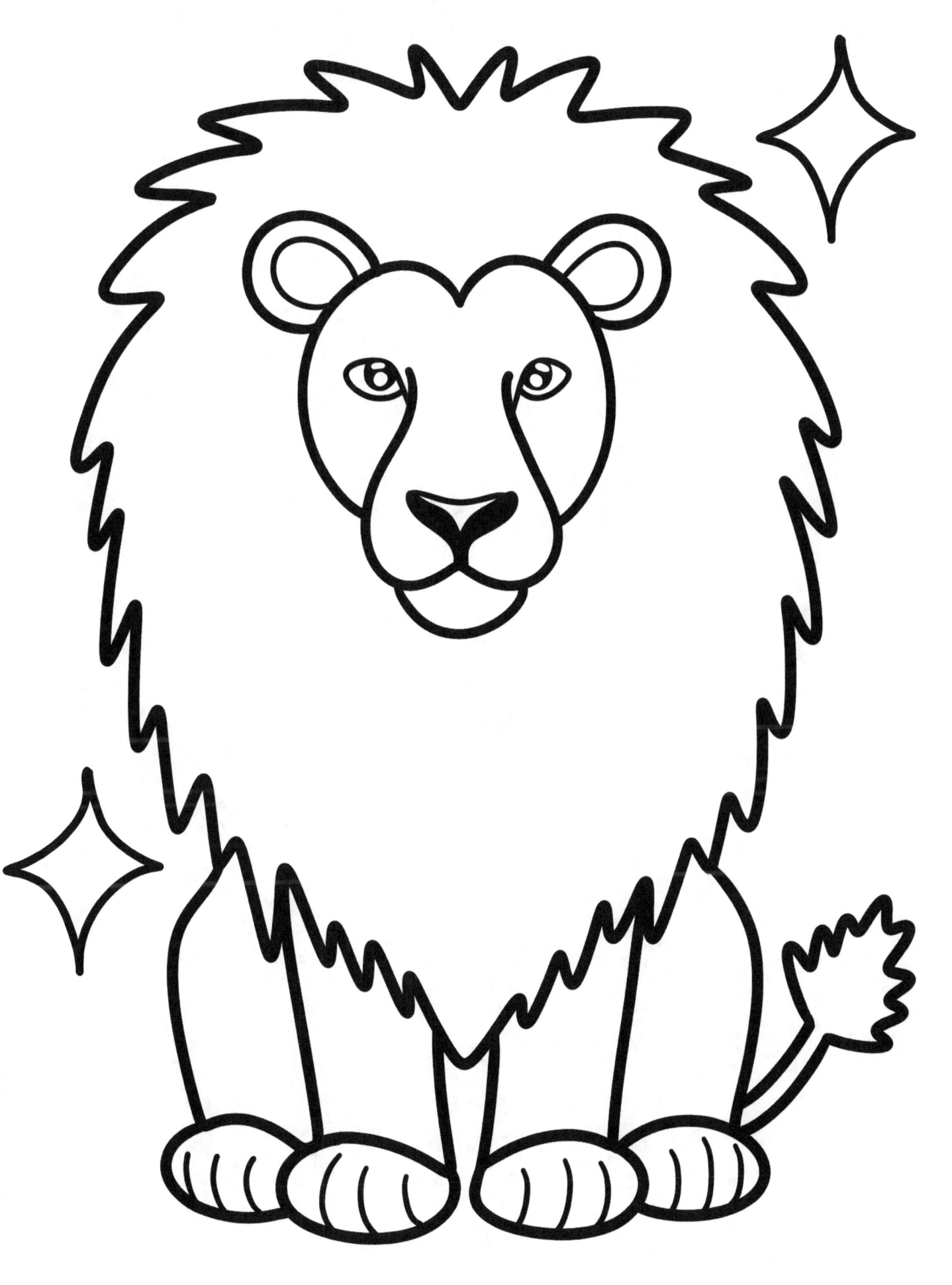

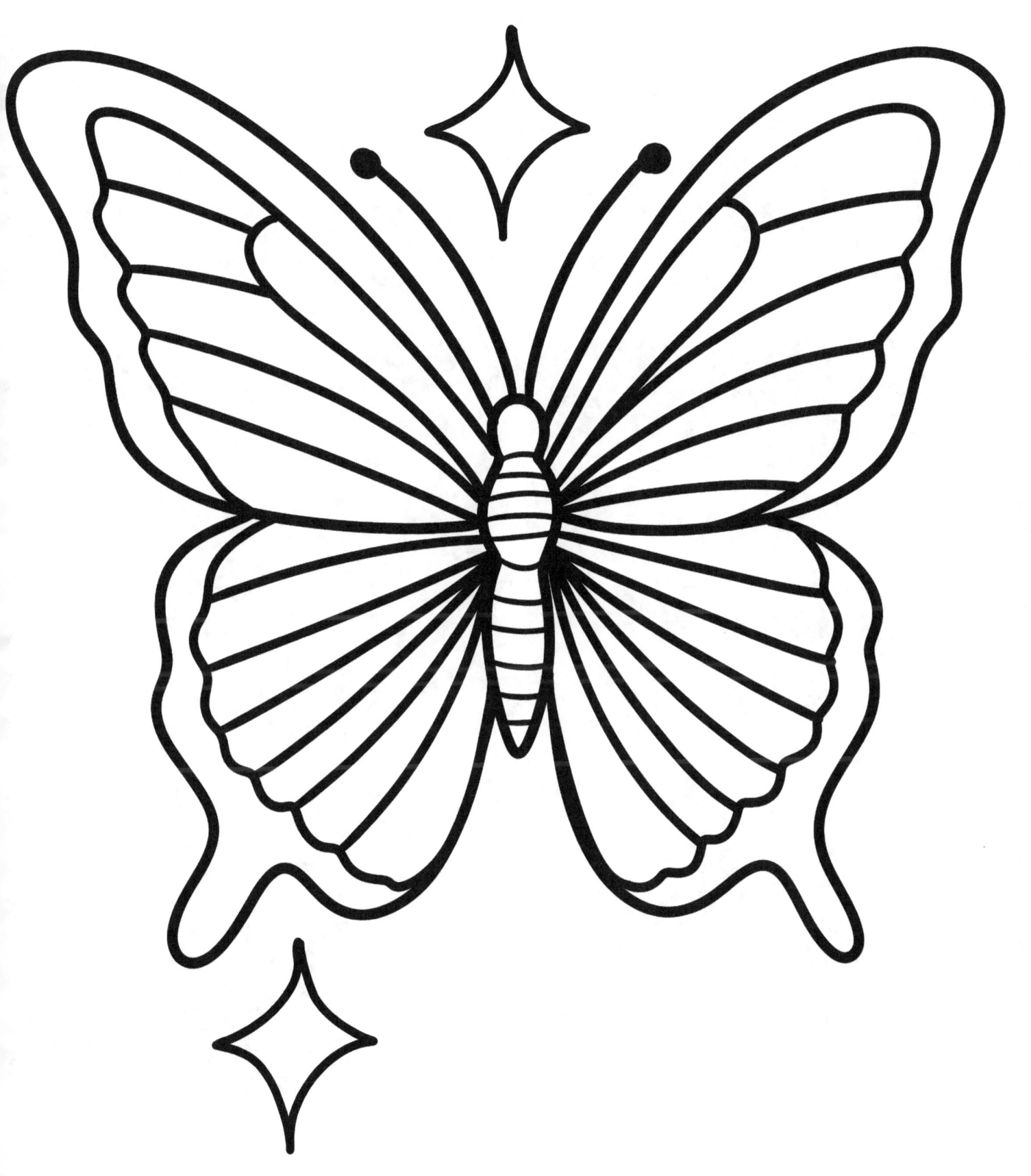

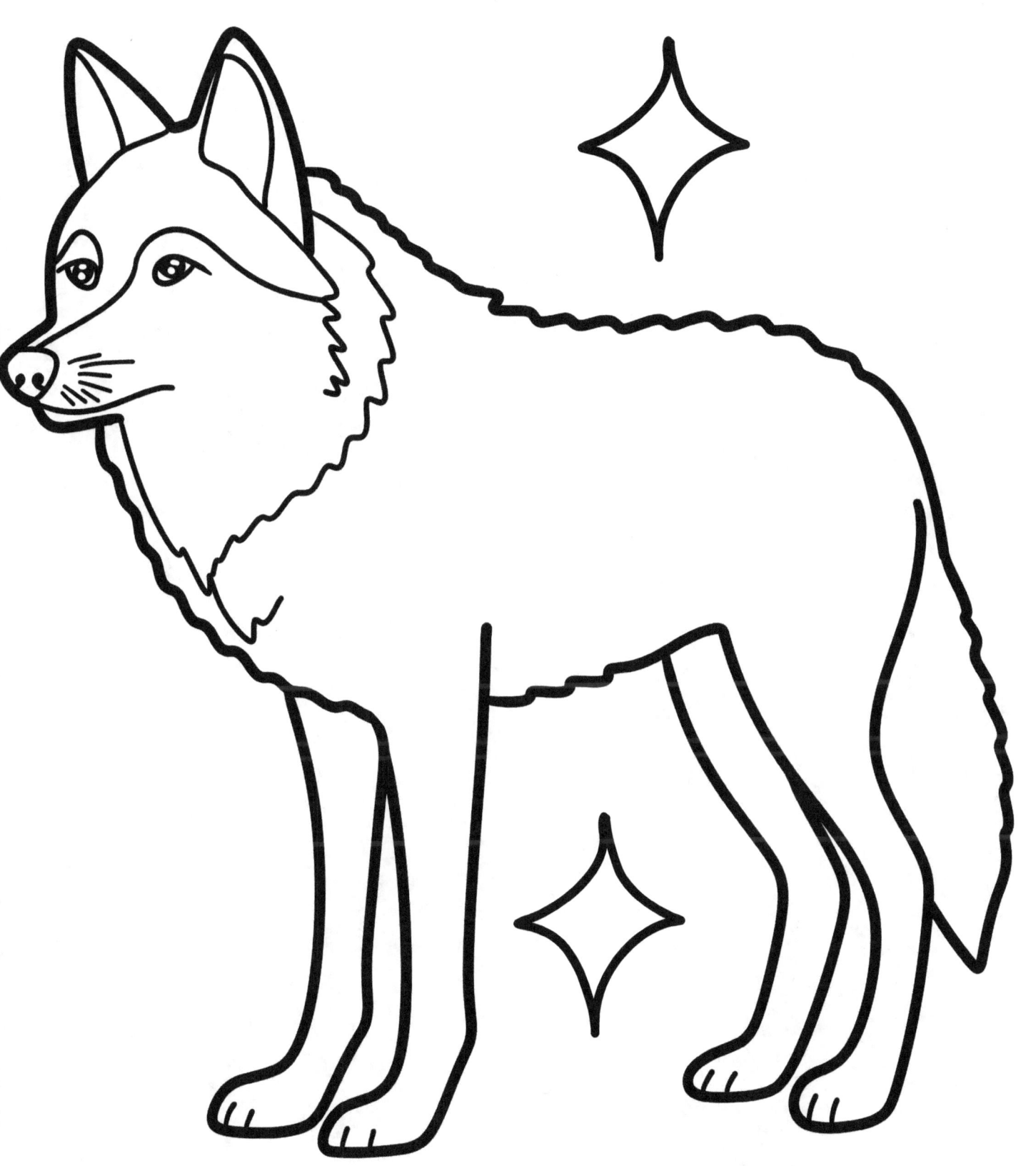

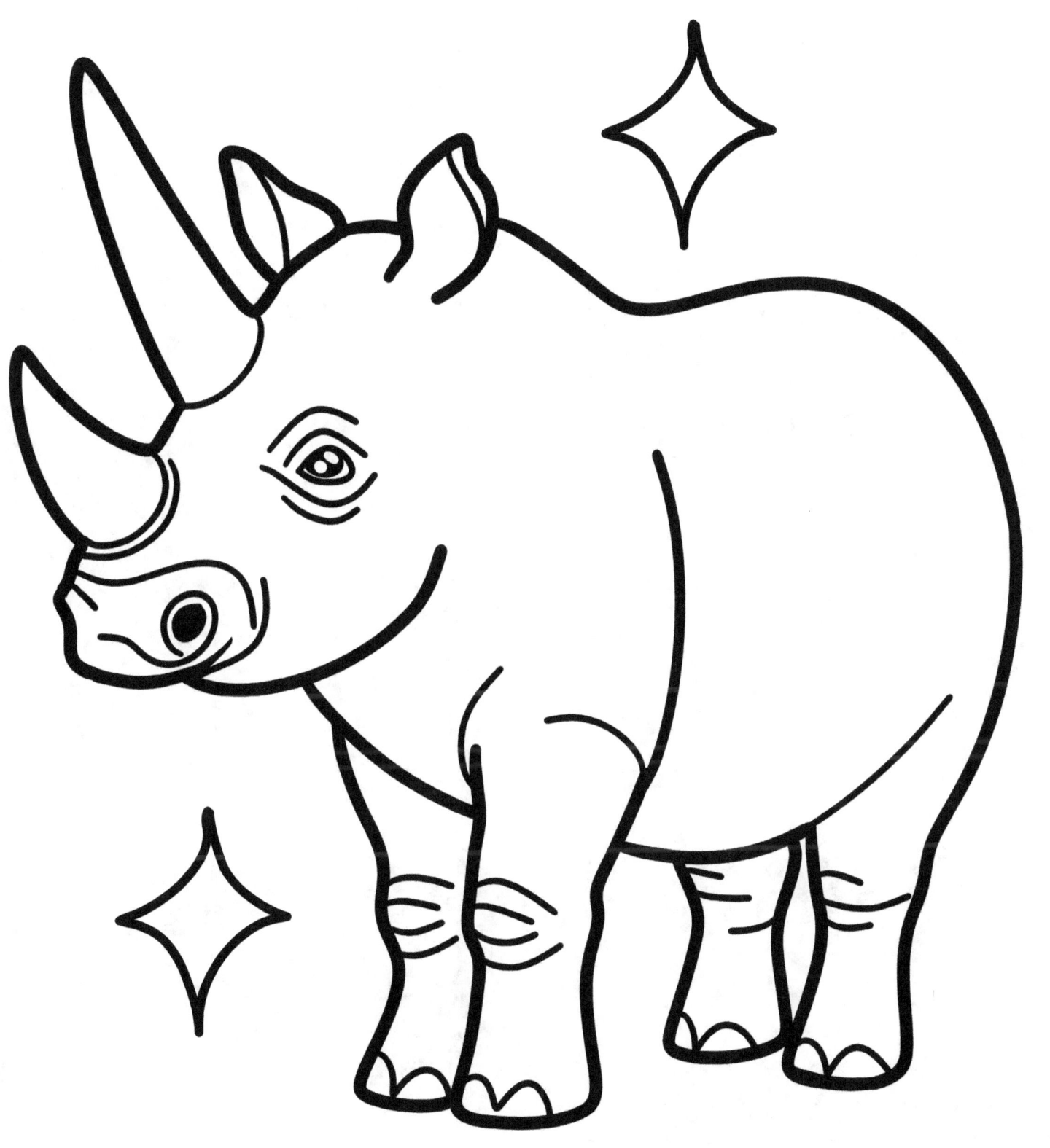

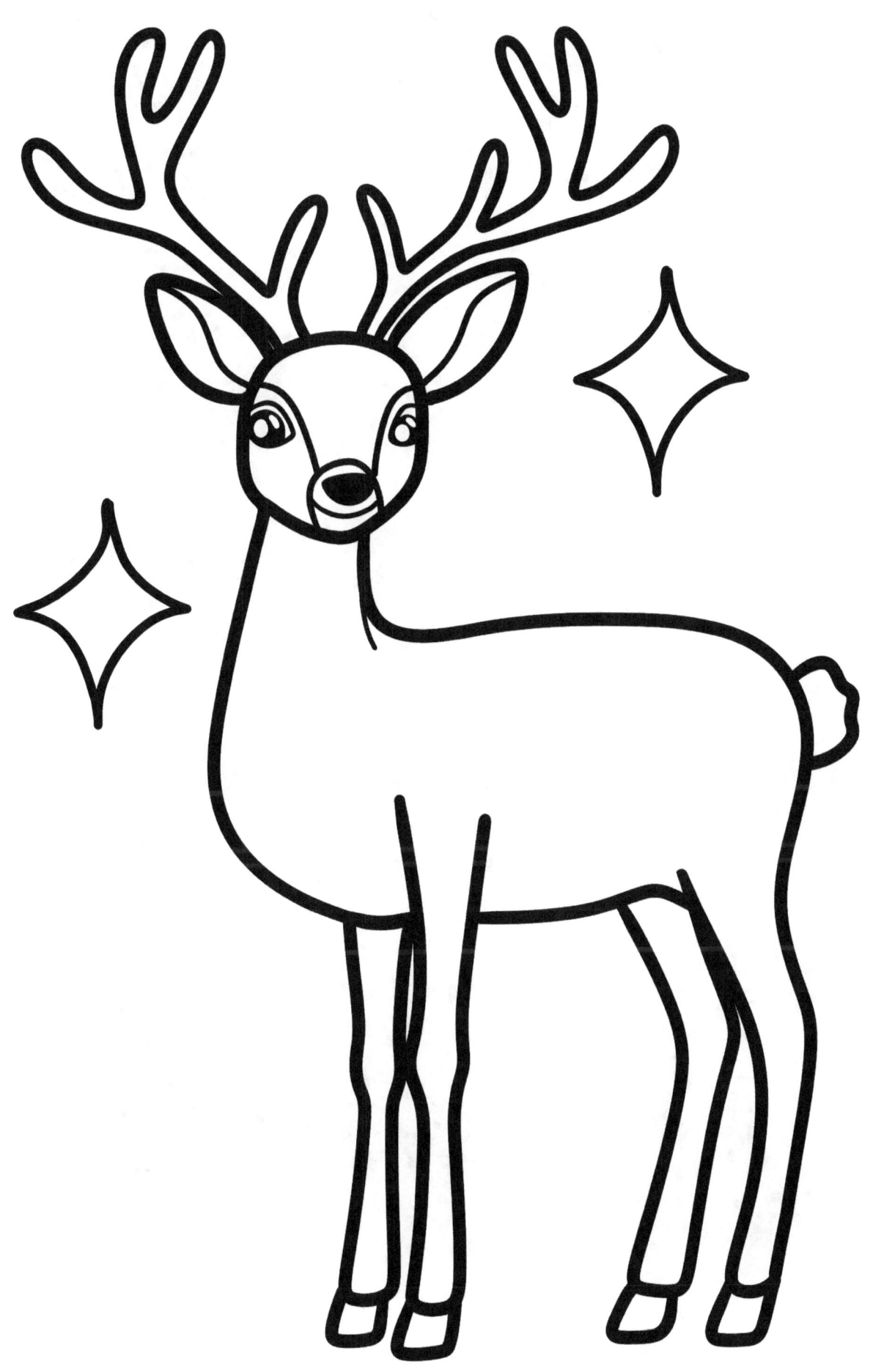

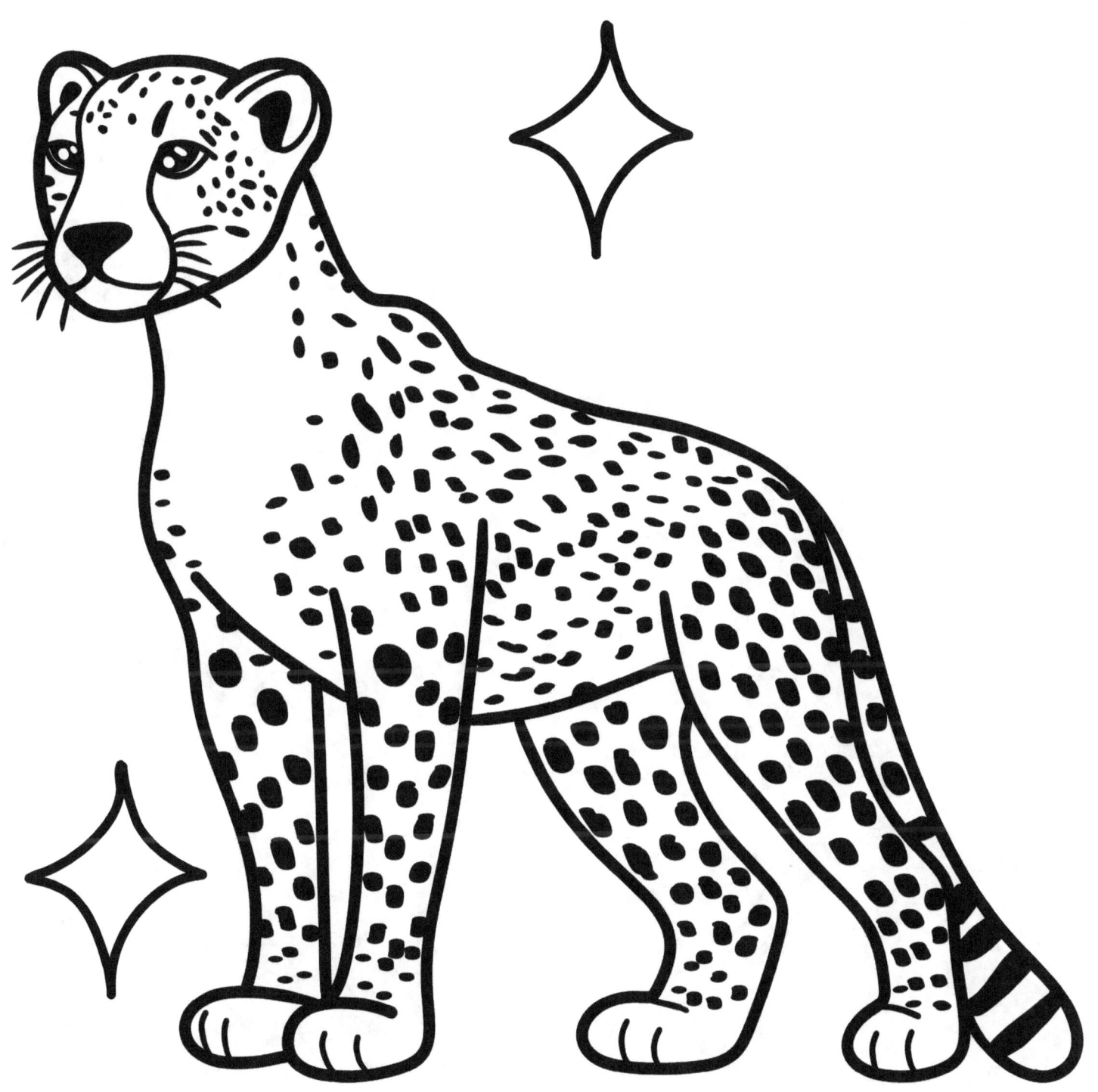

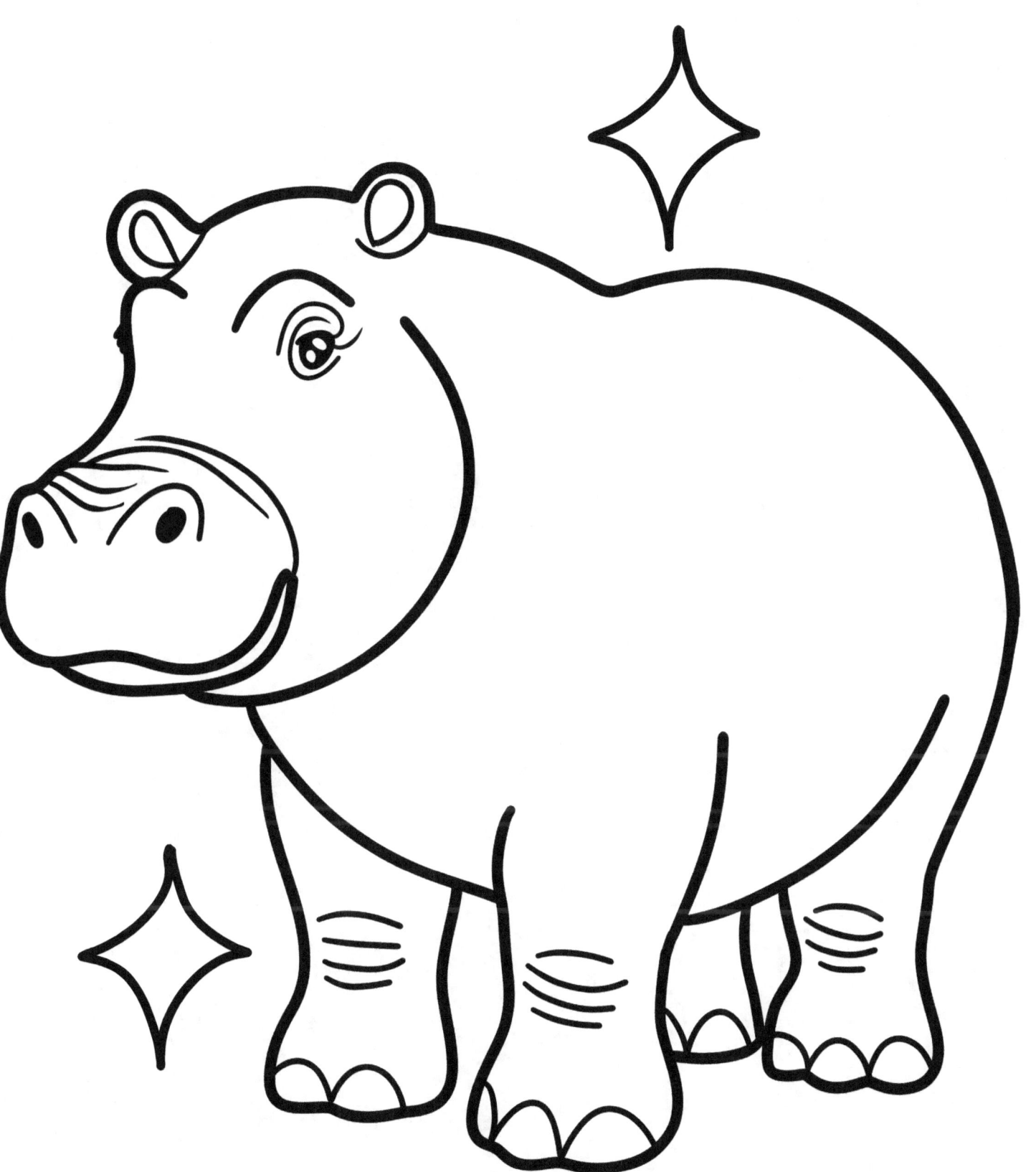

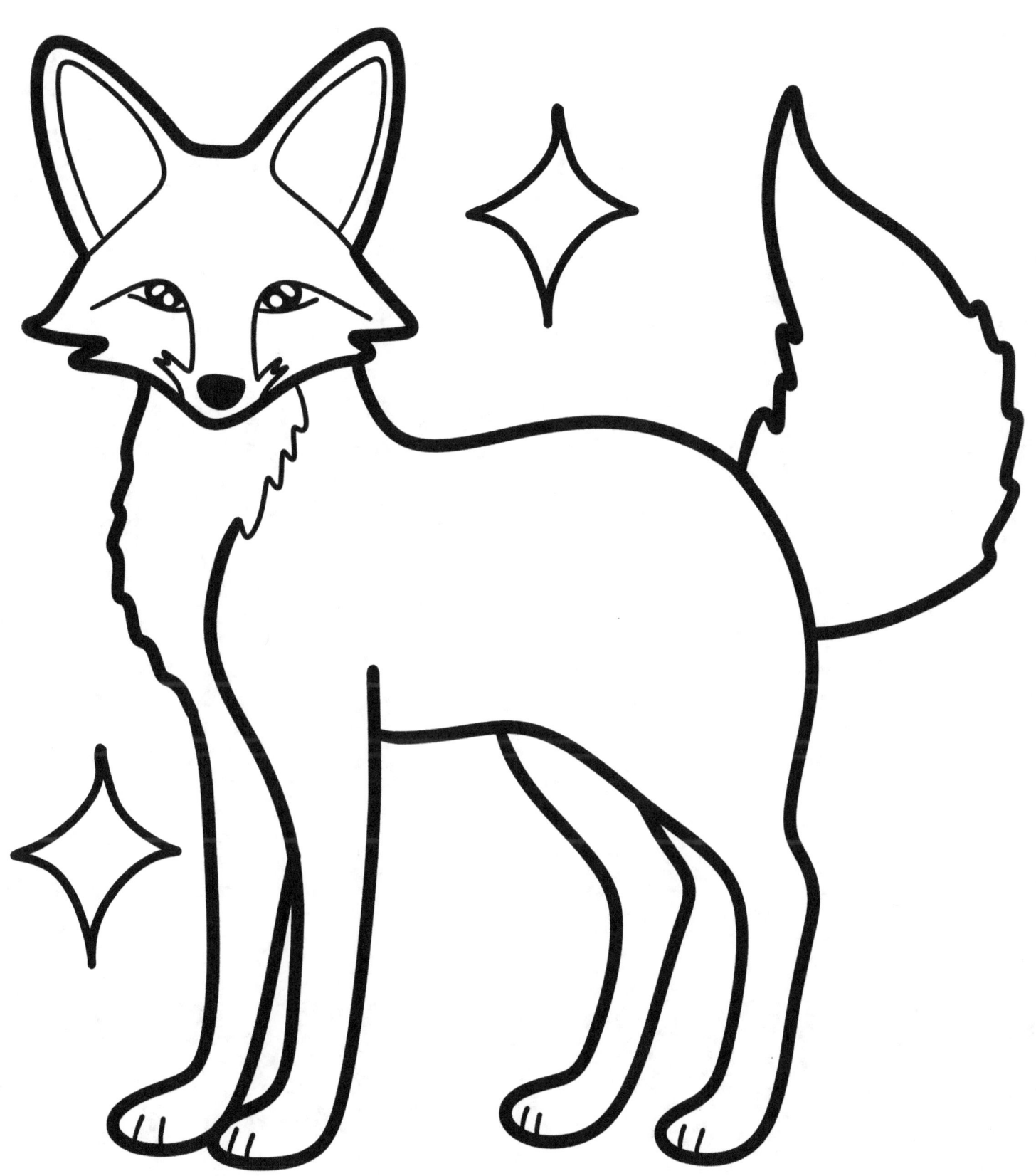

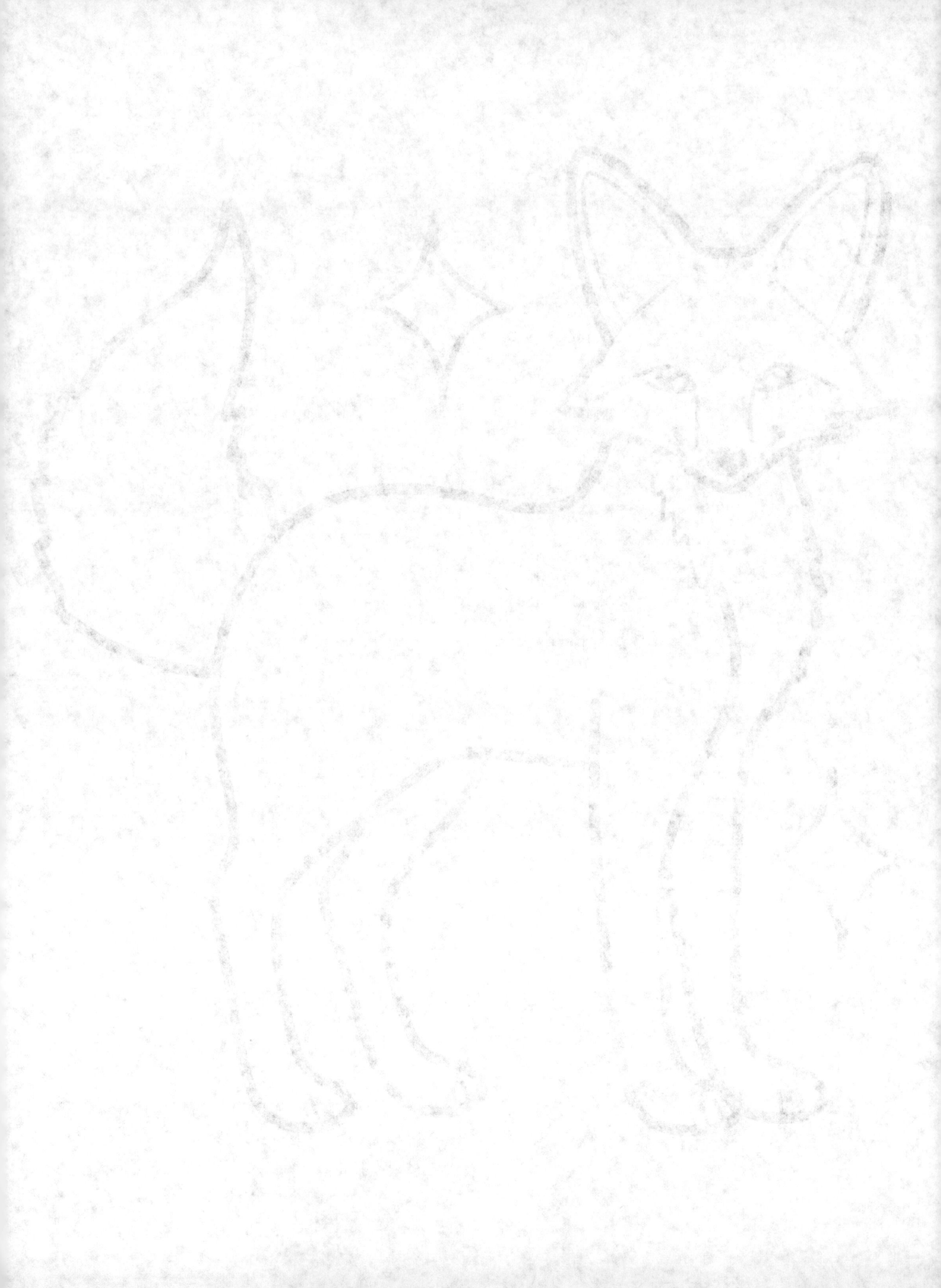

WE'D LOVE TO HEAR FROM YOU! YOUR FEEDBACK MEANS THE WORLD TO US AND HELPS CREARTDESIGN GROW. IF YOU ENJOYED THIS BOOK, PLEASE CONSIDER LEAVING A COMMENT OR REVIEW. YOUR THOUGHTS CAN INSPIRE OTHER COLORING ENTHUSIASTS AND HELP THEM FIND THE PERFECT BOOK FOR THEIR CREATIVE JOURNEY. THANK YOU FOR SUPPORTING OUR SMALL BUSINESS — WE TRULY APPRECIATE YOUR LOVE FOR COLORING!

SCAN THE QR CODE WITH YOUR CAMERA APP.
YOUR ACCOUNT WILL OPEN IN YOUR BROWSER.
SHARE YOUR THOUGHTS AND LEAVE A REVIEW ABOUT THE BOOK.

YOUR FEEDBACK HELPS US GROW AND GUIDES OTHER COLORING ENTHUSIASTS!

THANK YOU!

www.ingramcontent.com/pod-product-compliance
Lightning Source LLC
Chambersburg PA
CBHW080001230526

45470CB00008B/2827